THE
Archive Photographs
SERIES

BRISTOL TRANSPORT

This Leyland Octopus, XHT 893 built in 1956, is seen here being loaded at Bristol Docks (when they were still fully operational). E.W. Badman and Sons were a long-established Bristol road haulage company, dating back to horse-drawn days. In 1964 they sold out to Sparrows of Bath.

Compiled by
David Cheesley

First published 1998

The Chalford Publishing Company
St Mary's Mill, Chalford,
Stroud, Gloucestershire, GL6 8NX

ISBN 0 7524 1083 0

Typesetting and origination by
The Chalford Publishing Company
Printed in Great Britain by
Bailey Print, Dursley, Gloucestershire

This book is dedicated to the memory of my grandmother,
Mary Ann Osborne (1892-1970)

Contents

The author's favourite station - Lawrence Hill. British Railways 3MT Class 2-6-2T No. 82037 coasts into the station with a four-coach local from Severn Beach on 24 June 1961. The author spent many hundreds of hours train-spotting at this station when it still boasted a booking office, footbridge, four platforms, a signal box, waiting rooms and a goods yard with a large shed. Today, only two platforms remain and the only buildings are of a basic, 'bus-shelter', variety.

Acknowledgements

I would like to thank these people and organisations for their help in supplying photographs and information for this book: Barton Hill History Group, Bristol City Council, Bristol Reference Library, Bristol Evening Post, Bristol Vintage Bus Group, PSV Circle, The Omnibus Society, Ern Osborne, Ron Mojer, Mike Tozer, Dot Tranter, (the late) Fred Bond, Andy Jones, Peter Davey, (the late) George Timbrell, Jean Brake, (the late) Harold Dancey, Derek Fleming, (the late) H.C. Casserley, H. Priestley (with the permission of Paul and Jill Wilmot), Bernard Little, Mrs Lines, Roy King, Wally Webb, Jack Williams, Ray Petty, Phil French, Les Heron, Barry D'Cruz, Ivor Cheesley and Jean Cheesley.

I would especially like to thank Mike Tozer for allowing me to use photographs from his collection and Peter Davey for giving me access to his collection and the photographs taken by his late father, S. Miles Davey.

'Our Bus'. Close inspection reveals that the vehicle is Bristol Tramways C8113 (OHY 970), a Bristol KSW6B with standard Eastern Coach Works bodywork, built in 1953.

Introduction

Bristol is unique. Its history has probably been recorded in more books and publications than most other provincial cities. From the early days of photography, images of the changing Bristol scenes have been captured on camera and recorded for posterity. One man in particular, Reece Winstone, started to publish these pictures in books, the theme of each one being a certain period. This inspired others to take and collect pictures and the author of this book is one of them.

For many years now it has been my intention to produce a book of photographs of the changing Bristol transport scene. I know that there have been many railway books and several studies of trams and buses published, but no single work has embraced all forms of wheeled transport. Chalford have given me the opportunity to achieve this goal and realise this eclectic publication.

My interest in transport began with Bristol buses. As a child in the 1950s, travelling on buses was part of everyday life. Taking pride of place in my photograph collection is a picture of me, aged three, in a pushchair with my mother, about to board a number eight bus at Hareclive Road, Hartcliffe. The photograph was taken in 1955 and on the back is written 'Our Bus' (above). In 1956 we moved from Hartcliffe to Cadbury Heath. Route 311 was our lifeline to town and my grandmother and a journey was made there at least once a week. The route possessed much transport interest as it passed the Longwell Green coachworks, Hanham bus depot and Lawrence Hill station. School holidays were spent at grandmother's house in Wellington Road, St Pauls, which overlooked Joseph Fish's transport yard. I took great interest in the comings and goings of the Bedford lorries.

We moved again in 1963, this time to Redfield. My transport interest really developed at this time. Train-spotting at Lawrence Hill and Barrow Road marked the beginnings of a lifelong enthusiasm for railways. In 1965 I acquired my first camera and began to take pictures of the railways and buses of Bristol. In 1972, I attended my first steam engine rally at Hursley Hill, Whitchurch, which generated an interest in steam traction and fairground transport. Since then I have avidly photographed and collected pictures of all forms of road and rail transport with specific reference to Bristol.

One
Four-legged Friends

There can be no friendlier form of transport than the horse. Not only does he provide the power, but he is also a companion as well. Before the advent of the steam engine, horse-drawn vehicles fulfilled this country's main transport requirements. Roads did not exist as we know them today, being basically well-worn tracks. The road from Bristol to London only improved with the Turnpike Act of 1727, which made Turnpike trusts responsible for sections of road, in return for the payment of tolls. Tolls eventually became a great nuisance and the system was abolished in 1867. The invention of tarmacadam greatly improved road surfaces.

The changeover from horse to steam power was not instantaneous. Steam-driven road locomotives were slow and heavy and only suitable for moving very heavy loads. Horses remained ideal for local deliveries, whilst long-distance transport requirements were fulfilled by the railways. Only when the petrol engine arrived did horses begin to disappear in large numbers, the services they provided being taken over by small vans and lorries. Even then, in Bristol, George's Brewery and local rag and bone men carried on using the horse until the early 1960s.

The ultimate in horse-drawn transport: the Lord Mayor of Bristol's carriage. Here it is seen, complete with police escort, passing the Victoria Rooms, Queens Road on the way to a civic service.

This milepost is situated on the Bristol to Bath Road, at St George. It probably dates back to the turnpike days.

Bristol Corporation handcart used by the cleansing department. Carts such as this were made at the Bristol Wagon and Carriage Works at Lawrence Hill.

This is how people enjoyed a day out before motorised transport: a four-horse brake, seen near Newfoundland Road, around 1910.

A similar outing, photographed in Pennywell Road outside R. Willby's bakers shop, also around 1910.

A fine example of a baker's two-wheel, horse-drawn cart, *c.* 1905. This vehicle belonged to Rowlands Bakery of no. 1A, Verrier Road, Redfield.

Two horse-drawn delivery carts stand outside of J.H. Mill's grocery store at no. 4, Clarence Road, Lawrence Hill, *c.* 1905.

Horse-drawn delivery van belonging to J.K. Miles, house furnisher of Merchant Street, *c.* 1905.

Horse-drawn delivery cart belonging to Fry's Chocolate, used on local deliveries in Bristol from their factory at The Pithay, *c.* 1910.

W.J. Bence and Sons, coach builders and wheelwrights, had their works at Longwell Green. A brand new cart built for Bristol Stoneware Sanitary Co., coal and builders merchants of Lawrence Hill railway wharf, is seen here outside the works around 1910.

This four-wheeled cart, owned by the Bristol Co-operative Society, is all dressed up for a local parade, around 1900.

Jim Cox, sawdust dealer of St Philips, used this horse and cart. This picture was taken around 1920.

This coal cart was owned by Baldwin's and was based at Midland Road railway yard. The man with the horse is Fred Bond, who lived at Morley Street, Barton Hill. The photograph was taken around 1912.

George's Brewery always used grey horses for local dray-cart deliveries in the Bristol area. The horses and carts were always kept in pristine condition. Each year George's had an annual horse show at Hanham, to which staff, publicans and their families were invited. The fleet is seen here at the Bath Street brewery in the 1930s.

The Draycarts were painted dark green and, in later years, carried the famous grey horse symbol, also used on George's bottled beers. This cart has been preserved and can be seen in the Bristol Industrial Museum in the city docks.

Two

Steamers

The heyday of the steam road locomotive was between 1875 and 1945. The engines were built by famous names such as Burrell, Fowler, Foster, Garratt and Aveling and Porter.

I attended my first steam traction engine rally in 1972 and was immediately captivated by their sheer magnificence, in particular the showmen's versions with their twisted brass canopies and dynamos, but also the humble steamroller, which I remembered from my youth. Councils often hung on to these leviathans of the road long after they were obsolete. The smell of the tar, the rumble of the roller, the hissing of the steam and the occasional whistle, were sensations that generations of schoolboys remember fondly. Not to be forgotten in this class of vehicles were the steam wagons, favoured by local breweries. Georges, United and Rogers all had them. Sentinel produced some magnificent models, including eight-wheelers, but strict government regulations had killed off their development by the 1930s.

The fact that so many steam engines survive in preservation is a testament to their durability and the esteem in which they are held by enthusiasts.

Burrell 2072 'The Masterpiece', is believed to be the oldest surviving showman's road locomotive with original fittings. It entered service with John Cole of Staple Hill in March 1898 and travelled in Bristol and the West Country throughout its working life.

Steam fire engine, owned by the Bristol Police fire brigade, *c.* 1900.

Burrell showman's road locomotive, No. 3159. Built in December 1909 for Anderton and Rowland of Bristol. Originally it worked with a Bioscope show and later became a generator for the Venetian gondola ride. In 1932 it was sold to Plymouth showmen, T. Whitelegg and Sons, and toured the West Country with their American radio cars. In 1953 it was secured for preservation by fairground enthusiasts.

This steam lorry and trailer belonged to W.J. Rogers Ltd, brewers. Roger's bitter was marketed as 'AK'. The 'AK' symbol, inside a triangle, can be seen on the side of the lorry and trailer. The lorry had solid tyres, was chain driven and appears very similar to vehicles built by the Bristol Wagon and Carriage Works at Lawrence Hill in the 1900s.

Steam lorry built by the Bristol Wagon and Carriage Works, c. 1904.

This Foden steam wagon belonged to the works fleet of the Bristol Tramways and Carriage Co. Ltd. It was registered, by Foden, in Cheshire and carries the number M1864. The Motor Car Act of 1903 had required that, from 1 January 1904, every motor vehicle should be assigned a registration mark. In the early years it was common practice for many commercial vehicles to be registered locally by their makers.

Another Foden steam wagon, also registered in Cheshire, was M3569, owned by Davey and Co. Ltd, removal and haulage contracters. It could travel at an amazing five mph and carry eight tons of goods!

AW3978 was registered in Salop before delivery, by Sentinel (whose works were in Shrewsbury), to Bristol removal and haulage contractors Joseph Fish and Sons Ltd, around 1918. Joseph Fish was an old established Bristol company, based at nos 111-117 Victoria Street. Their vehicles were painted in a dark green livery.

Fry's Chocolate used this Super Sentinel four-wheel steam lorry and trailer in the mid 1920s.

George's Brewery had a fleet of ten Super Sentinels for long distance deliveries. The fleet is seen here lined up at the Bath Street brewery during the mid 1920s. Note 'George's Bristol Beers' painted proudly on the front of the steamers.

The steamroller was an everyday sight until the early 1960s. YD973 was built by Aveling and Porter in 1930 and was owned by W.W. Buncombe of Highbridge, Somerset. It is now preserved and is seen here at Frocester Manor Steam Rally on 28 May 1984 in the ownership of C.H. Hawkins of Staple Hill, Bristol. It appears at rallies all around the Bristol area, towing a wooden caravan as it did during its working days.

Three

God's Wonderful Railway

The Great Western was unique amongst railways. An icon to its employees, no other railway commanded so much respect. The GWR was established in Bristol during 1835 to build a line to London. Financed by Bristol businessmen, its great engineer, Isambard Kingdom Brunel, designed a remarkable railway: from the impressive bridges and buildings, all constructed along neo-classical lines, to the widened track gauge, larger locomotives and more spacious carriages than any other company that had gone before.

The GWR did everything in its own way and considered this way superior to any other. Through acquisitions and amalgamations, the GWR spread far and wide from Bristol. Temple Meads station was the hub of the railway. Express trains from London, the Midlands and the South West rubbed shoulders with cross-country trains to Weymouth and Cardiff as well as local services to Portishead, Radstock and Severn Beach. Temple Meads goods depot sent items, manufactured by Bristol based industries, all over the country. Marshalling yards at East Depot and Stoke Gifford kept wagons rolling twenty-four hours a day.

Great Western Railway's magnificent 'King' Class locomotive 6024, *King Edward I*, makes a triumphant return to the Bath Road depot on 4 April 1994 following its renovation. Before this, the engine had spent years rusting away at Woodham's scrapyard on Barry Island.

The frontage of Isambard Kingdom Brunel's original Great Western Railway station, built between 1839 and 1841. It was designed in a Tudor revival style and had offices across the end that faced the road with the engine shed behind and then the passenger shed behind that. The station was opened when the GWR line to London was completed in 1841. Engines were turned around on turntables and moved from line to line in the engine shed. This station is the most complete surviving example of an early provincial terminal.

The approach to Bristol Temple Meads station, *c.* 1910. On the left is Brunel's original station. In the middle is the entrance to the new station, built between 1865 and 1878 and designed by Sir Matthew Digby Wyatt for the GWR and the Midland Railway. The later buildings were also built in a mock-Tudor style and featured a large, curved main roof on the train shed. To the extreme right of the picture are the Bristol and Exeter Railway offices, built during 1852 in a Jacobean style. In the foreground is AE1847, a Bristol Tramway's blue cab.

Bristol Temple Meads station, decorated for the coronation of Queen Elizabeth II in June 1953. On the right is a Bristol Tramways single decker, C2728 (JHT863), on route seventeen to Temple Meads. The bus is a 1947 Bristol L5G with ECW dual-doorway bodywork. It was sold to Hong Kong in 1960. The three black cars on the right are probably taxis.

Bristol Temple Meads station, looking east from the westward end, *c.* 1925. A footbridge links the platforms under the main shed roof. Between 1930 and 1935, the station was modified by P.E. Culverhouse. The footbridge was removed and replaced by through roads. New platforms were added outside of the train shed. These possessed cream-coloured terracotta buildings which had 'BRISTOL' written on them in glazed letters.

'Castle' class locomotive, No. 5059 *Earl St Aldwyn*, being oiled at the east end of Temple Meads station around 1960. The wagons behind are being shunted into the busy goods depot. The engine will be taking over an express that has come up from the West of England.

Train-spotters pack the end of platform twelve at Temple Meads. All eyes are on 'Hall' class 6972, *Beningbrough Hall*, as it pulls in. Another express waits on the other side of the platform. Platform twelve had a good view of the comings and goings at the Bath Road shed: hence its popularity with train-spotters.

'Hall' class 6935 *Browsholme Hall*, at Bath Road depot, *c*. 1952. In the background can be seen the heavy-lifting shop and the fuelling stage, with the water tank above. The shed buildings at Bath Road were built in 1934 and its GWR shed code was BRD. Under British Railways, the shed became 82A and, on 1 January 1948, eighty-seven locomotives were allocated to it. The shed closed to steam in September 1960.

Panoramic view of Bristol Temple Meads goods depot, *c*. 1960. When it was opened in 1924, it was the largest covered goods shed in the world. The lines to the left ran down to Bristol Docks and were part of the Bristol Harbour lines. The old signal box in the middle was removed in the late 1970s.

During the early 1930s, Bristol Temple Meads' station lines and signalling system were modernised. Old-fashioned semaphore signals were replaced with coloured lights and new signal boxes were built at each end of the station. In this picture, track relaying is still taking place in front of the new east signal box; two 28XX class locomotives stand side by side. A steam crane is at work with a large contingent of permanent way men. When it was opened in 1935, Bristol Temple Meads' East signal box was the largest on the GWR, boasting some 368 levers.

The entrance to the railway yard at Queen Ann Road, Barton Hill, 1972. Before the Second World War, horses and cattle were loaded and unloaded from trains here.

38XX class 2-8-0 No. 3863 waits behind another 2-8-0 28XX class at the large fuelling stage at St Philip's Marsh depot. St Philips Marsh was the second largest shed on the GWR. It was opened in July 1910 and, on 1 January 1948, had 141 locomotives allocated to it. Its GWR shed code was SPM and this became 82B under British Railways. Its main purpose was to supply freight locomotives for the Bristol division and engines for local branches. It closed in June 1964 and the engines were transferred to Barrow Road.

'Castle' class 4087 *Cardigan Castle*, at the head of a group of locomotives at St Philips Marsh depot, 9 February 1964. The engine has obviously been withdrawn, as it is minus nameplates and some fittings and the chimney is covered with sacking. In the background can be seen the shed housing the two turntables.

Unidentified 'Hall' class passing East Depot with an express train, 24 August 1958. Both up and down yards look busy. This was Bristol's main marshalling yard with shunting continuing both day and night.

55XX class 2-6-2T No. 5536 pauses at St Anne's Park with a Bath to Bristol local passenger train, 24 August 1958. All the buildings and platforms of this once-picturesque station have been demolished. Nowadays there is no trace that a station ever existed here.

Special promotion train at Fry's Somerdale Factory, *c.* 1935. The Great Western engine is a 57XX class 0-6-0PT, remarkably dressed up for occasion with special headboard and flags. The Lord Mayor looks on as Fry's girls wave to the photographer.

Great Western charm: this is a fine example of a rural halt, complete with typical pagoda hut, but is actually situated on the outskirts of a big city, this one being at Whitchurch on the Bristol to Radstock and Frome branch.

One of the most impressive signal gantries in Bristol was situated here, at Dr Day's Bridge Junction, Barton Hill. In this picture, a Hymek diesel hydraulic, D7050, pilots 'Hall' class 5974 *Wallsworth Hall* on the 2.30pm Cardiff to Portsmouth train, 22 June 1963. The picture was taken during the changeover from steam to diesel. All the houses above the embankment have since been demolished, although the block of flats, 'Harwood House', remains standing to this day.

The line at Lawrence Hill station was often subject to flooding. This is the approach to the station on one such occasion in the 1960s: the line is under four feet of water.

Lawrence Hill station was opened in 1863 by the Bristol and South Wales Union Railway. Trains ran via New Passage to a ferry until 1886, when the Severn Tunnel was opened. In 1891 the station was rebuilt. The entrance was situated at road level, concrete steps leading down to the platform. This picture was taken on 26 May 1970, just prior to demolition.

Lawrence Hill also had a fine signal box, built in 1891. When this photograph was taken, on 26 May 1970, coloured light signals are in place and the box is about to be made redundant, all signals from this time being worked from the new panel box at Temple Meads. In the background can be seen the Midland line, which crossed Lawrence Hill just north of the box and the Bristol Greyhound depot.

G. W. R.

On SATURDAYS, Dec. 2nd and 16th.

English League. Second Division.

Bristol City

v.

HUDDERSFIELD TOWN	GLOSSOP,
DECEMBER 2nd.	DECEMBER 16th.
KICK-OFF 2.30 p.m.	KICK-OFF 2.30 p.m.

N.B—In the event of either match being postponed or abandoned, the special facilities announced on the bill will not be given.

SUBURBAN TRAINS WILL RUN TO AND FROM

ASHTON GATE

PLATFORM (Adjoining the Bristol City Football Ground)

AS UNDER:

NORTH AND EAST SUBURBAN TRAINS.

To Ashton Gate.

		December 2nd and 16th.
		P.M.
CLIFTON DOWN	...dep.	1 † 39
REDLAND ...	„	1 † 41
MONTPELIER	... „	1 † 43
STAPLETON ROAD	„	1 50
LAWRENCE HILL	„	1 55
TEMPLE MEADS ...	„	1 * 53
BEDMINSTER	... „	2 6
ASHTON GATE	...arr.	2 13

* Change at Bedminster. † Change at Stapleton Road on forward journey.

From Ashton Gate.

		December 2nd and 16th.
		P.M.
ASHTON GATE	dep.	4 25
BEDMINSTER	arr.	4 29
TEMPLE MEADS	„	4 36
LAWRENCE HILL	„	4 42
STAPLETON ROAD	„	4 45
MONTPELIER	„	4 51
REDLAND	„	4 54
CLIFTON DOWN	„	4 56

For particulars of Fares, see other side.

For Train service from and to Portishead Branch see other side.

Great Western Railway handbill of 1911 that gives details of football specials running to Ashton Gate from other Bristol suburban stations.

Stapleton Road was Bristol's second station. As well as being the junction for Clifton and Avonmouth, many Cardiff to Portsmouth trains called only at Stapleton Road (this was to avoid having to reverse, as they would have had to in Temple Meads). In this early 1900 view, the station is adorned with some fine enamel signs and appears to be doing good business with milk traffic.

Heavy freight locomotive 28XX class 2-8-0 No. 2869, storms Ashley Hill Bank at Narroways Hill, laden with Salisbury to South Wales freight, 20 July 1933. Most heavy freight trains required a banking engine. On the right, the joint Great Western and Midland line to Avonmouth and Severn Beach begins. The field on the left later contained a giant gas holder.

John Lysaght's had its own private railway system at Netham Works which linked with the Great Western Railway at the Bristol East depot. In this view, 0-4-0ST No. 19 poses with its crew. The engine was built in 1918 by Hawthorn Leslie (works no. 3333). The plate on the engine reads 'JLL No. 19' and the photograph was taken in 1934.

A very large piece of steelwork waits to leave John Lysaght's Netham Works mounted on a special Great Western Railway wagon called a 'pollen'. The wagon will be tripped to the East depot by one of the JL 0-4-0STs. The works had thirteen acres of extensive workshops and sorting yards and boasted an overhead crane in addition to the standard gauge tank and crane engines.

Great Western Railway goods depot at Canons Marsh adjoining the large railway yard. The depot was built in the shadow of Bristol Cathedral and handled vast amounts of freight traffic to, and from, Bristol Docks. In 1914 the depot handled 500 wagons every day.

Inside Canons Marsh goods depot, shortly after construction in 1906, as empty wagons await loading. The steelwork was constructed by John Lysaght's and this picture was featured in a works' catalogue. The destinations of the wagons can be seen chalked on the main stantions. Transfer trips worked the wagons to outlying marshalling yards.

'Warship' class diesel hydraulic D835 *Pegasus* at Temple Meads station. During 1960, this class began replacing steam locomotives in the Western Region. All engines in the class were named after famous Royal Navy warships. This author has a special affection for this particular locomotive, as it was the first of the class he ever saw.

The 'Western' class diesels were more powerful and were introduced in 1961. Western Class diesel hydraulics D1048 *Western Lady*, rolls into Temple Meads with the IM85 Plymouth to Manchester express during December 1974. The Western class engines are regarded by many enthusiasts as the finest-looking diesel locomotives ever built.

Other Western Region diesel hydraulic types were the Hymek, North British and Paxman. The smallest of these was the Paxman, designed to replace pannier tanks on branch and local goods trains. Almost as quickly as they were introduced during 1964, the work they were designed for disappeared. D9537, seen here, was built in 1965 and is now preserved by the Gloucestershire and Warwickshire Railway at Toddington.

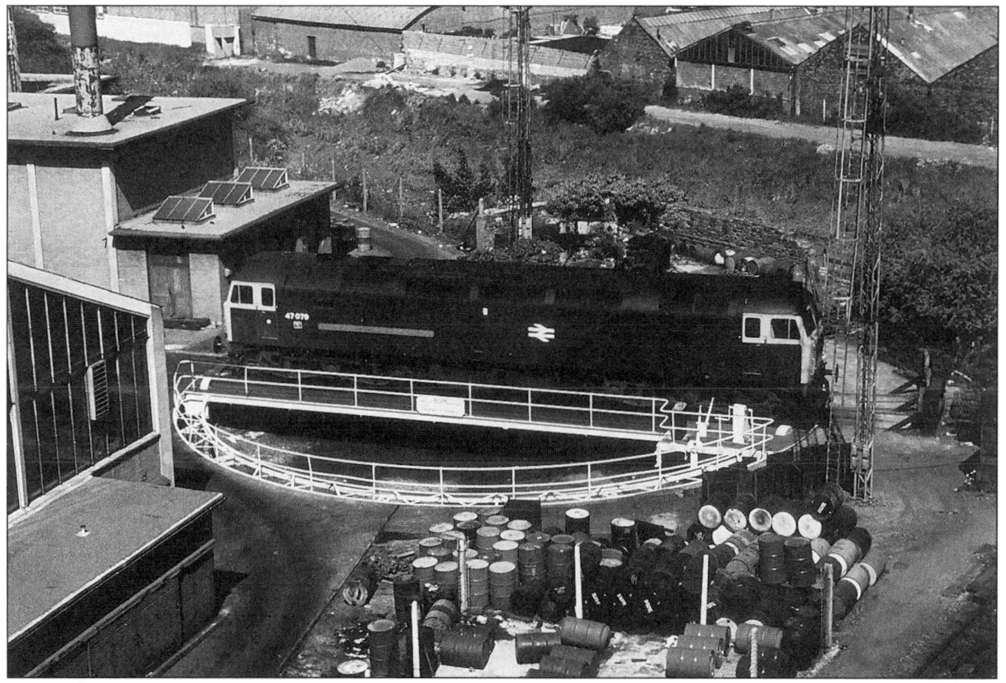

In 1962 the Brush Type 4 diesel engines were introduced. The Western Region locomotives included seventeen named after former Great Western Railway chief mechanical engineers and famous board gauge engines. 47079 *George Jackson Churchward* is seen here on the turntable at the back of Bath Road diesel depot on 22 May 1977. The engine's original number was D1664.

During the 1970s, all local coal yards in Bristol were closed and coal was concentrated in two depots. The main one was at Wapping Wharf with another at Filton. This engine, No. 2736 *Western Pride*, is shunting the yard at Wapping Wharf under the ownership of Western Fuel on 19 May 1978.

No. 2736 rests at Wapping Wharf depot, 14 October 1980. The loaded coal hoppers were tripped everyday from Ashton Bridge to Wapping Wharf by British Rail locomotives. The Western Fuel engine then shunted them into the coal depot for unloading. The depot was closed during the 1980s and is now a car park.

Four

Midland Outpost

Bristol's other railway was the Midland Railway. Although it did not have the same grand title as the Great Western and the engines were not as impressive, its employee's were fiercely loyal. If the GWR did things one way, then the Midland did it the other. Midland men hated the GWR and even today when old railwaymen get together they will argue over which railway was the best.

The origins of the Midland line in Bristol began with a horse tramway that opened in 1835 between Coalpit Heath and Avonside Wharf to transport coal. In 1839 the line was absorbed by the Bristol and Gloucester Railway and was extended to Gloucester in 1844. Ten years later it became part of the Midland Railway and ran as far as Birmingham. The Midland built a large engine shed and extensive sidings at Barrow Road. The line closed in 1970 and has now been turned into a cycleway. Today, only a short siding to the council refuse disposal plant, built in 1985, remains.

The year is 1965 and these are the last days of steam at the former Midland Railway shed at Barrow Road: only two steam engines can be seen here. A GWR 'Hall' class 4-6-0, ambles past, devoid of its brass numbers and nameplates, with its numbers just chalked on the cab door. Resting in the background is 8F 2-8-0 No. 48046. Also in the background, a three-car diesel multiple unit heads up the Midland main line with a Bristol to Worcester train.

This signal box was located at the approach to Barrow Road sheds from Temple Meads and was known as the Engine Shed Sidings signal box. It was a standard Midland Railway box that stood between the main line and the wagon repair works. The box remained until the late 1970s. The wagon repair works remains and is now the Bristol depot of the privatised English, Welsh and Scottish Railways. This image was captured on 30 September 1973.

Midland Railway 1P class 0-4-4T No. 1267, rests in the sunshine at Barrow Road during May 1935. The wooden steps in the background were replaced with concrete ones in 1938. A coal wagon is on the line loading to the wooden stage on the other side of the bridge – which was also replaced with a concrete structure in 1938.

Midland Railway 3F 0-6-0 No. 3181 stands inside the roundhouse at Barrow Road on 20 April 1934. The engine looks very clean, with a nicely polished dome and seems to be receiving careful attention of some kind. The Midland Railway was a small engine railway that favoured the 0-6-0 wheel arrangement for goods traffic. However, this often meant double-heading for heavy trains.

This is a fascinating selection of engines around the turntable in the Barrow Road roundhouse, 27 May 1935. On the left is class 4P compound 4-4-0 No. 1030 (then the largest on the line) and in the middle is 3F class 0-6-0 No. 3173. To the right can be seen 1P 0-4-4T No. 1228.

The lines alongside Barrow Road are packed with steaming locomotives as 'Jubilee' class 4-6-0, No. 45594 *Bhopal*, rushes down the Midland line with an express from the north. The lower quandrant signal in the centre is an original Midland Railway signal. Many of these on the Midland line were replaced with LMS signals, which were upper quadrant.

A fine sight at Barrow Road, sometime in the late 1950s, is this 'Patriot' Class 4-6-0 No. 45506 *The Royal Pioneer Corps*. Behind can be seen the gasworks at Days Road, which always dominated the shed and the wall by the bridge over which countless schoolboys had slid in order to bunk across the shed. Sometime in the early 1960s the foreman had the wall coated in oil to stop this practice.

The famous concrete steps at Barrow Road, built in 1938 to replace the original wooden ones. I wonder how many railwaymen and train-spotters have walked up and down here? The author first pushed open the wooden door at the top in the summer of 1965, the last year of steam, to take a glimpse of the panoramic landscape of sheds (seen below).

Steam and smoke all around you: this was the view of Barrow Road from the concrete steps. What we would have given to have lived in those houses at Digby Street on the left. Imagine being able to watch trains from your bedroom! 'Black 5' Class 4-6-0, No. 45272, and other engines simmer and hiss in the sunshine as another 'Black 5' coasts past the shed with an express train.

To the north of the shed were carriage sidings and then the extensive Midland Road goods yard. In between was the line that ran down to Avonside Wharf. An LMS 'Jinty' can be seen departing in the background. To the left can be seen a Midland Railway brake van and, behind that, the shunters office and mess room.

After taking water it is time for a break. This late 1950s scene shows a group of young railwaymen resting whilst No. 47552 simmers alongside. This was the height of the teddyboy era, as can be seen by the hairstyles.

During 1938 and 1939, coal and ash plants were built at Barrow Road. On the left is an ash-handling plant of ferro-concrete construction. On the right is the coal plant, which had a pair of seventy-five ton bunkers. This busy scene, taken in the late 1950s, includes 'Crab' 2-6-0 No. 42771, a 'Patriot' 4-6-0 and a 'Jinty' 0-6-0T. The houses in the background were all demolished in the early 1960s to make way for 'Baynton House' and 'Kingsmarsh House': two multi-storey blocks of flats.

The line to Avonside Wharf required engines with small driving wheels, due to sharp curves at the Avon Street end. Towards the end of steam, the Pug 0-4-0STs used on the line were replaced by British Railways 03 Class diesel shunters. Here D2188, sporting its original green livery, stands by the shunter's mess hall in March 1966, after the Barrow Road shed had closed.

The Avonside line crossed two roads: Barton Road and Avon Street. The Barton Road crossing is pictured here on 3 April 1954. It had a lovely pedestrian footbridge. In the background can be seen Kingsland Road bridge, which took a lot of traffic over the railway. The lines that can be seen in the foreground fan out into the goods yard and then continue to Avonside Wharf. In later years, Blue Circle cement built a depot at the Wharf and other traffic including molasses, which ran to the distillery in Avon Street, and scrap metal from various yards in the area were also transported from here.

Staff of St Philips station pose on the single platform in 1953. The wooden building suffered a disastrous fire in later years. The Midland Railway had originally held big plans for this station but went on to develop Temple Meads, in conjunction with the Great Western Railway, instead. Local trains ran from St Philips to Bath Green Park. The station opened in 1870 and closed to passengers in 1953. The goods service lasted until 1967.

The pride of Barrow Road, Jubilee class 4-6-0 No. 45690 *Leander*, storms the incline to Fishponds, over the Great Western South Wales line at Lawrence Hill in the late 1950s, with a train of 'blood and custard' coaches behind. To the left can be seen Lawrence Hill goods yard with its lines of coal wagons. The Bristol to Mangotsfield line closed on 3 January 1970 and is now a cycleway.

Severn Beach station. This image will conjure up happy memories to Bristolians over the age of forty. The station was opened in 1923 and there was a determined effort by the Midland Railway to promote Severn Beach as a resort. Throughout the Midlands, Severn Beach was promoted as the 'Blackpool of the West'. Local trains ran from Severn Beach to Bristol, either via Avonmouth or Pilning low level. The buildings seen here have all been demolished since this was taken.

Most goods yards had their own local coal merchants. At Clifton Down it was L. Twining and Co. Ltd. The workforce is shown here in front of a pre-war Ford three-ton dropside, sometime around 1953. From left to right: Ernie Davis (sat in cab), Johnny Lomax, Tom Coles, Arthur Knowles, Aubrey Lomax and Pat Payne. Behind them is a 1952 Bedford O-type whilst houses in St Johns Road can be seen behind this. On the right, hidden by the mound of coal, is the start of the tunnel under Clifton Down.

Before the Second World War, local coal merchants owned their own wagons. These were mainly ten-tonners, like this one which is in the livery of Ocean (a large South Wales colliery). The author's father, Ivor Cheesley, is pictured here. He worked for local coal merchants E.E Mills, H.E. Coole and also the Coal Agencies Ltd, during the 1940s. All these merchants owned their own wagons.

The Port of Bristol Authority operated its own fleet of steam engines on over seventy miles of track within the Avonmouth Dock area. Up to twenty locomotives were employed. This photograph, taken on 31 May 1931, shows 'Peckett' Class 0-6-0ST *Fyffe* at the Avonmouth Dock shed. The name illustrates how important the banana trade was to Avonmouth, as it required trains of special vans.

The Port of Bristol Authority built a new engine shed at Avonmouth in 1950. In 1965 the last steam engines were replaced by a fleet of Sentinel diesel shunters. *Portbury*, *Henbury* and a Fox Walker engine were stored in the shed until their move to Bristol Industrial Museum. Traffic in the docks gradually declined until the depot's closure in the early 1980s and all the Sentinels were sold. This view of the depot was taken after closure and it looks a sorry sight.

Bristol built many fine industrial steam locomotives: Fox Walker, Avonside and Peckett became famous names throughout the country. All steam locomotives carried maker's plates and this fine example is on Peckett No. 1976, built in Bristol at the Fishponds works in 1939. It survives to this day at Toddington on the Gloucestershire and Warwickshire Railway.

In 1961 the first diesel electric locomotives arrived on the Midland Line and soon took over express passenger duties from the 'Jubilee' class trains. The diesels were the 'Peak' class, so-called because the first ten were named after British mountains. Eventually, the 'Peaks' took over practically all duties on the line. When the Midland Line closed in 1970, 'Peaks' still remained in Bristol, on express, freight and parcels trains. Here, 45144 *Royal Signals* (originally numbered D55), runs past Bath Road diesel depot, 25 May 1985.

Five

Electric Sparks

I am not old enough to have known Bristol's trams and yet they have always held a fascination for me. Ever since I can remember, I have cut out pictures of them when they have appeared in local newspapers. I think it must have been because my grandmother and other older people always talked about them with such enthusiasm. Even though they were antiquated, uncomfortable and uncovered they always looked pristine and were reliable. There were also family connections with this charismatic form of transport. My great-uncle, Walt Cheesley, was a tram driver at the St George depot and another close relative, Bill Heath, was a driver at the Eastville depot. Bill enthralled me with many stories of his days on the trams and the characters with whom he worked.

The fact that no Bristol electric tram has survived will always be a source of annoyance to local transport enthusiasts. Some good models do exist and, hopefully, one day a full-scale replica may be built.

Tramways Centre, 10 September 1937. This driver, in summer uniform, takes a break, standing in front of car No. 206. Behind, car No. 223 can be seen on the Westbury route. Advertisements on the trams are for companies which include: Avon tyres, Jones' department store and Ristol motor oil.

A young Bristol Tramways conductor poses for the camera at a studio in the early 1900s. The heavy serge overcoat has brass buttons which have 'BTCCL' stamped on them. The cloth badge on the cap says: 'BTCCL Conductor'.

Bristol's first electric tramway route was from Old Market to Kingswood. This photograph was taken at the Kingswood terminus on 14 October 1895, as various dignitaries posed with car No. 92. The opening of the electric tramway was a great occasion.

Bristol Tramways and Carriage Co. Ltd, used this horse-drawn wagon for overhead work on the tramway system. This image was captured in around 1900.

The electric tramway offered a safe and reliable service between Old Market and Kingswood and led to the development of the suburbs that grew up between the two. Soon after the line was opened, this tramcar was photographed at Old Market, loading in the middle of the cobbled road. The conductor is wearing a uniform reminiscent of those worn by soldiers fighting in the American Civil War.

Other electric routes soon followed and the hub of the system became the Tramways Centre. In this picture from the 1930s, car No. 94 heads for Westbury whilst No. 211 awaits its next trip to Hotwells. Advertisements on the trams advertise Ty-Phoo tea, Swan Vesta matches and Harris sausages.

The Tramways Centre in all its magnificence, with the company offices on the left, 1937. In the middle is 'Skivvies Island', so-called because this was where young female domestic servants met their boyfriends on their days off. Tram lines surround the island. The trams would be operational for only four more years after this photograph was taken.

Three Bristol Tramway workers pose aboard No. 196 on the route between Hanham, Old Market and Bushy Park, around 1910. The crew and tram work from the St George depot and the picture must have been taken in summer because of the white tops to the caps. The drivers were completely exposed to the elements at all times and could become practically frozen during the winter!

St George tram depot buildings. The depot was opened in October 1876 for horse trams working the Old Market to St George line. A horse-bus feeder operated from the fountain to Kingswood. A power station was built at the back of the depot and, on 14 October 1895, the first electric trams ran from Old Market to Kingswood. The depot was used as an AFS depot during the Second World War and then as a transport depot, before becoming a store for the Bristol Museum. In the 1980s it was demolished and sheltered flats have been built on the site. The author's Ford Cortina, AWS 595V, is pictured here parked outside the depot shortly before it was demolished.

Bristol Bridge and High Street, *c*. 1902. A tram car passes a horse-drawn cart on the bridge, whilst two trams pass one another by the Samuel Morley statue. Large river trows are drawn up at the bridge. Advertisements for Birchell's pianos and The Old Post Office tea can be seen on the sides of the vehicles.

Car No. 164 sits in the sunshine on Durdham Downs before another journey back to Eastville. Advertisements are for George's beers and Harris' sausages.

Six o'clock in the evening at Old Market during the summer of 1935. Five trams are in view and these include cars Nos 16, 173 and 212. All trams were loaded in the middle of the road. It is nearly the end of the rush hour but the policeman is still on duty controlling traffic. An approaching lorry, belonging to John Hodgson Junior, can be seen.

Old Market, rush hour, late 1920s. The passengers have formed two large queues, but the inspector is clearly in control.

Car No. 193, on route from Hanham to Old Market, climbs Bryants Hill. Car No. 193 was allocated to the St George depot and carries an advert for Regent Super petrol on its front. The author's uncle, Walt Cheesley, was a driver on this route and lived not far from here in Church Road, Hanham. It was on this route that he met his future wife.

The end of the journey for the Old Market to Hanham route was outside the Bristol Tramways bus depot in Hanham High Street. Here, the crew of car No. 192 pose for the cameraman before returning to Old Market. Car No. 192 carries an advertisement for Dunlop tyres whilst car No. 194 sports an advert for Regent Super petrol. This is somewhat ironic as both products were essential to the trams' main competitor and eventual successor, the motor bus.

The last rites for Bristol trams were conducted at the Kingswood depot. A hole was knocked through the back of the depot and a line was laid through leading to two sidings on waste ground. The trams were then pushed through one by one as they were withdrawn, between May 1938 and April 1941. The cars were then stripped and burnt. One of the last survivors, car No. 132, is pictured here awaiting its fate in the summer of 1941.

The Clifton Rocks Railway opened on 11 March 1893 and linked Hotwells with Clifton by way of a vertical-inclined, water-powered cliff railway. The unusual thing about the Clifton line was that it was completely within a tunnel. The original frontage of the lower station can be seen in this view, taken around 1895. The Clifton suspension bridge can be seen in the top left-hand corner.

The Clifton Rocks Railway was designed by George Newnes and had four cars which worked in pairs. The cars boasted a smart blue and white colour scheme. The cars had many elaborate safety features. In 1912 Bristol Tramways acquired the Rocks Railway and it closed in 1934.

View of the top station with the four loading bays, three members of staff and the middle control office. All the power for the line was supplied by water and gravity. During the Second World War, the Clifton Rocks Railway tunnel was converted into an emergency radio studio for the BBC. However, it was never used and has been derelict since that time.

Six

White Coats and Mystery Tours

Bristol's first charabancs were delivered to Bristol Tramways in 1906. They became very popular after the First World War, when they replaced the horse-drawn wagonettes as the vehicle of choice for Sunday school, works and pub outings.

The charabanc was little more than a large car with many seats. It was open to the elements, had solid tyres and little suspension. A canopy could be pulled over in the case of inclement weather. Speed was restricted to twelve mph, yet it took people farther afield for the day than any horse-drawn vehicle could: Weston, Bath races and Cheddar were common destinations. Later, pneumatic tyres were fitted and vehicle reliability improved and trips to Weymouth, Minehead and Bournemouth became popular.

In the 1930s the more modern-looking motor coach appeared. Designs varied between the forward control of Bedford and Austin and the half-cab favoured by Leyland and AEC. However, the real heyday of coach travel was in the 1950s. Car ownership was not yet common at this time and the motor coach was the principle form of transport for day trips and holidays.

AEC charabanc HT3785, with solid tyres, seen here with a Bristol Co-operative Society dairy department outing, c. 1922.

A Daimler charabanc belonging to Greyhound Motors. In the early 1920s, Greyhound were Bristol Tramways' main competitors. This vehicle is Greyhound No. 3 (HT756), built in 1920, with solid rubber tyres.

Greyhound Motors had offices at no. 96, West Street, Old Market, with a depot just around the corner in Trinity Street, Newtown. The depot is still standing and is the last remaining original building in the area. When Greyhound were absorbed by Bristol Tramways in 1936, the depot passed to the Tramway Company, who used it until the 1970s. Since then it has been used as a tyre and exhaust centre. This picture was taken around 1985.

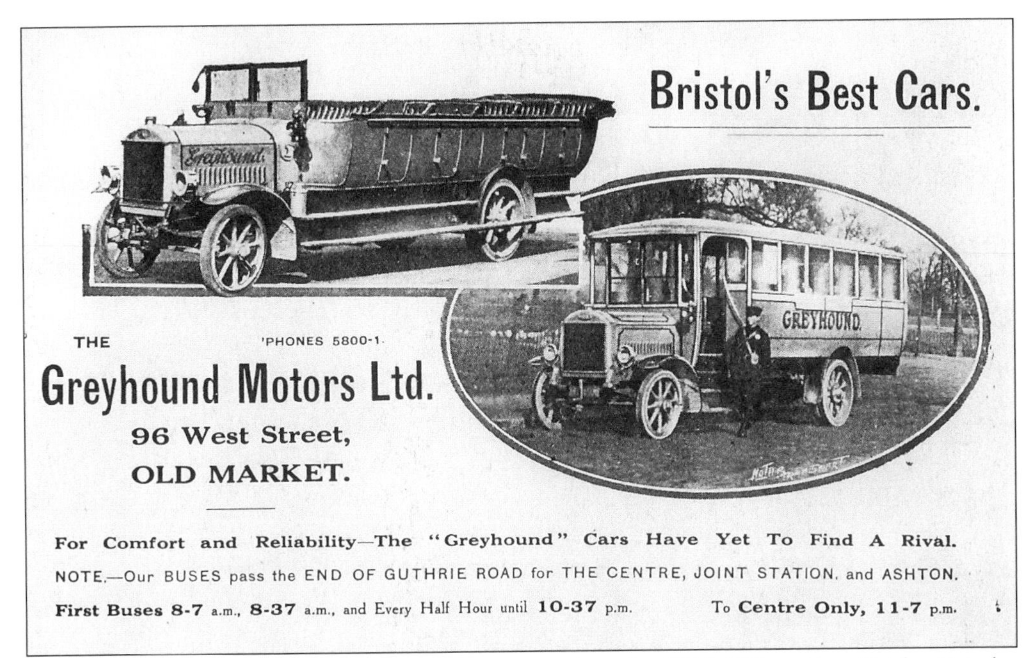

Advertisement for Greyhound Motors that appeared in the 1925 Clifton Zoo Guide. Daimler charabanc No. 2 and an early Daimler bus are illustrated.

On 10 February 1925, Greyhound Motors commenced a daily Bristol to London coach service (via Chippenham), using solid-tyred Dennis coaches. Taken in the 1930s, this photograph shows Greyhound No. B343 (HW3644), a Bristol type-B built in 1928, outside the Bristol Tramways Road Travel Bureau in Prince Street.

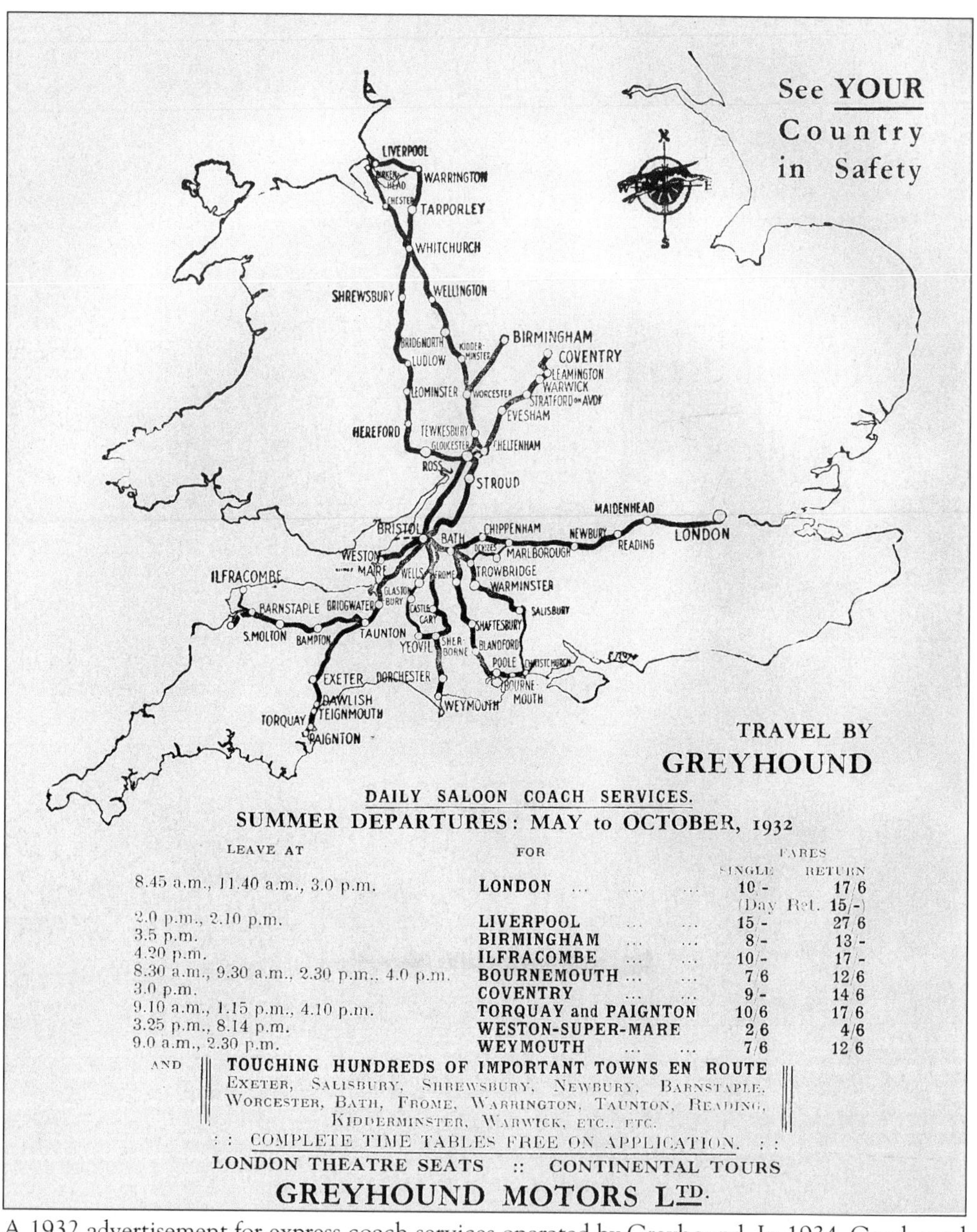

A 1932 advertisement for express coach services operated by Greyhound. In 1934, Greyhound became a member of Associated Motorways, pooling its services with other express operators, to provide even more destinations. Associated Motorways was later to become the main constituent company of National Express.

Bristol Tramways charabanc AE2797 outside 'The Glasshouse' public house at Lawrence Hill. Charabanc trips were very popular, a frequent jaunt being to Gough's Caves at Cheddar.

As well as the fleet of coaches acquired from Greyhound Motors, Bristol Tramways also operated its own fleet. BHU637, fleet number 2056, a Bristol JJW built in 1935, was fitted with a second-hand Duple body in June 1942. This picture was taken shortly after the end of the Second World War.

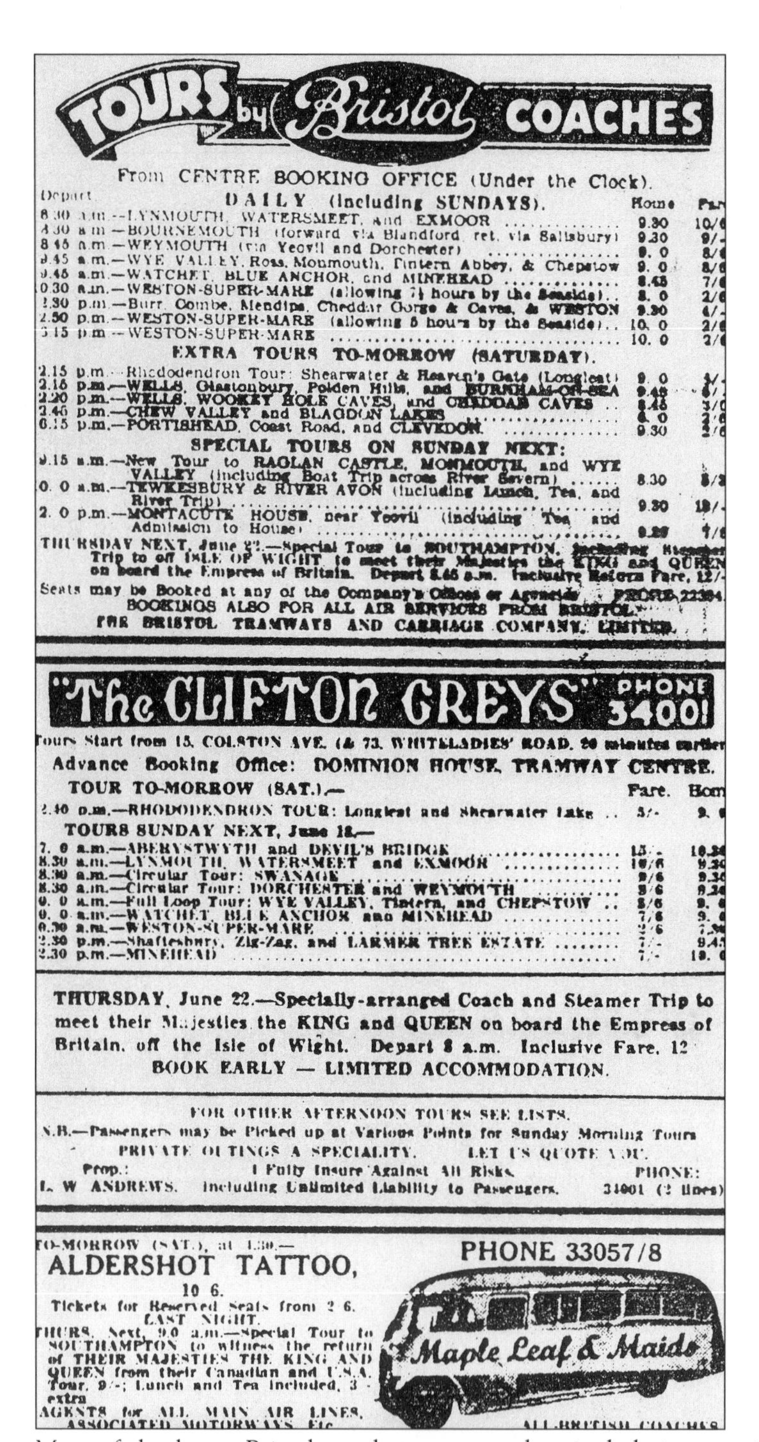

TOURS by Bristol COACHES

From CENTRE BOOKING OFFICE (Under the Clock).

DAILY (Including SUNDAYS).

Depart — Home — Fare

8.30 a.m.—LYNMOUTH, WATERSMEET, and EXMOOR 9.30 10/6
8.30 a.m.—BOURNEMOUTH (forward via Blandford, ret. via Salisbury) 9.30 9/-
8.45 a.m.—WEYMOUTH (via Yeovil and Dorchester) 9. 0 8/6
9.45 a.m.—WYE VALLEY, Ross, Monmouth, Tintern Abbey, & Chepstow 9. 0 8/6
9.45 a.m.—WATCHET, BLUE ANCHOR, and MINEHEAD 8.45 7/6
10.30 a.m.—WESTON-SUPER-MARE (allowing 7½ hours by the Seaside).. 8. 0 2/6
2.30 p.m.—Burr. Combe, Mendips, Cheddar Gorge & Caves, & WESTON 9.30 4/-
2.50 p.m.—WESTON-SUPER-MARE (allowing 5 hours by the Seaside).. 10. 0 2/6
3.15 p.m.—WESTON-SUPER-MARE 10. 0 2/6

EXTRA TOURS TO-MORROW (SATURDAY).

2.15 p.m.—Rhododendron Tour: Shearwater & Heaven's Gate (Longleat) 9. 0
2.15 p.m.—WELLS, Glastonbury, Polden Hills, and BURNHAM-ON-SEA 9.45
2.20 p.m.—WELLS, WOOKEY HOLE CAVES, and CHEDDAR CAVES .. 8.45 3/0
3.45 p.m.—CHEW VALLEY and BLAGDON LAKES 8. 0
6.15 p.m.—PORTISHEAD, Coast Road, and CLEVEDON 9.30

SPECIAL TOURS ON SUNDAY NEXT:

9.15 a.m.—New Tour to RAGLAN CASTLE, MONMOUTH, and WYE VALLEY (including Boat Trip across River Severn) 8.30
10. 0 a.m.—TEWKESBURY & RIVER AVON (including Lunch, Tea, and River Trip) 9.30
2. 0 p.m.—MONTACUTE HOUSE, near Yeovil (including Tea and Admission to House) ....

THURSDAY NEXT, June 22.—Special Tour to SOUTHAMPTON, including Steamer Trip to off ISLE OF WIGHT to meet their Majesties the KING and QUEEN on board the Empress of Britain. Depart 8.45 a.m. Inclusive Return Fare, 12/-

Seats may be Booked at any of the Company's Offices or Agencies. PHONE 22304.
BOOKINGS ALSO FOR ALL AIR SERVICES FROM BRISTOL.
THE BRISTOL TRAMWAYS AND CARRIAGE COMPANY, LIMITED.

"The CLIFTON GREYS" PHONE 34001

Tours Start from 15, COLSTON AVE. (& 73, WHITELADIES' ROAD, 20 minutes earlier)
Advance Booking Office: DOMINION HOUSE, TRAMWAY CENTRE.

TOUR TO-MORROW (SAT.)— Fare. Home

2.40 p.m.—RHODODENDRON TOUR: Longleat and Shearwater Lake .. 5/- 9. 0

TOURS SUNDAY NEXT, June 18.—

7. 0 a.m.—ABERYSTWYTH and DEVIL'S BRIDGE 15/- 10.30
8.30 a.m.—LYNMOUTH, WATERSMEET and EXMOOR 10/6 9.30
8.30 a.m.—Circular Tour: SWANAGE 9/6 9.30
8.30 a.m.—Circular Tour: DORCHESTER and WEYMOUTH 9/6 9.30
9. 0 a.m.—Full Loop Tour: WYE VALLEY, Tintern, and CHEPSTOW .. 8/6 9. 0
9. 0 a.m.—WATCHET, BLUE ANCHOR and MINEHEAD 7/6 9. 0
9.30 a.m.—WESTON-SUPER-MARE 2/6
2.30 p.m.—Shaftesbury, Zig-Zag, and LARMER TREE ESTATE 7/- 9.45
2.30 p.m.—MINEHEAD 7/- 10. 0

THURSDAY, June 22.—Specially-arranged Coach and Steamer Trip to meet their Majesties the KING and QUEEN on board the Empress of Britain, off the Isle of Wight. Depart 8 a.m. Inclusive Fare, 12
BOOK EARLY — LIMITED ACCOMMODATION.

FOR OTHER AFTERNOON TOURS SEE LISTS.
N.B.—Passengers may be Picked up at Various Points for Sunday Morning Tours
PRIVATE OUTINGS A SPECIALITY. LET US QUOTE YOU.
Prop.: L. W. ANDREWS. I Fully Insure Against All Risks, including Unlimited Liability to Passengers. PHONE: 34001 (2 lines)

TO-MORROW (SAT.), at 1.30.—
ALDERSHOT TATTOO,
10 6.
Tickets for Reserved Seats from 2 6.
LAST NIGHT.
THURS. Next, 9.0 a.m.—Special Tour to SOUTHAMPTON to witness the return of THEIR MAJESTIES THE KING AND QUEEN from their Canadian and U.S.A. Tour, 9/-; Lunch and Tea included, 3/- extra
AGENTS for ALL MAIN AIR LINES, ASSOCIATED MOTORWAYS, Etc.

PHONE 33057/8

ALL-BRITISH COACHES

Most of the larger Bristol coach operators advertised their tours in local newspapers. The advertisements in the *Bristol Evening Star* of 16 June 1939 are for Bristol Tramways' 'The Clifton Greys' and 'Maple Leaf and Maids'. This was the last summer of coach tours before the Second World War and the suspension of all tours until the summer of 1945. In 1947, both 'The Clifton Greys' and 'Maple Leaf and Maids' became part of Wessex Coaches Ltd.

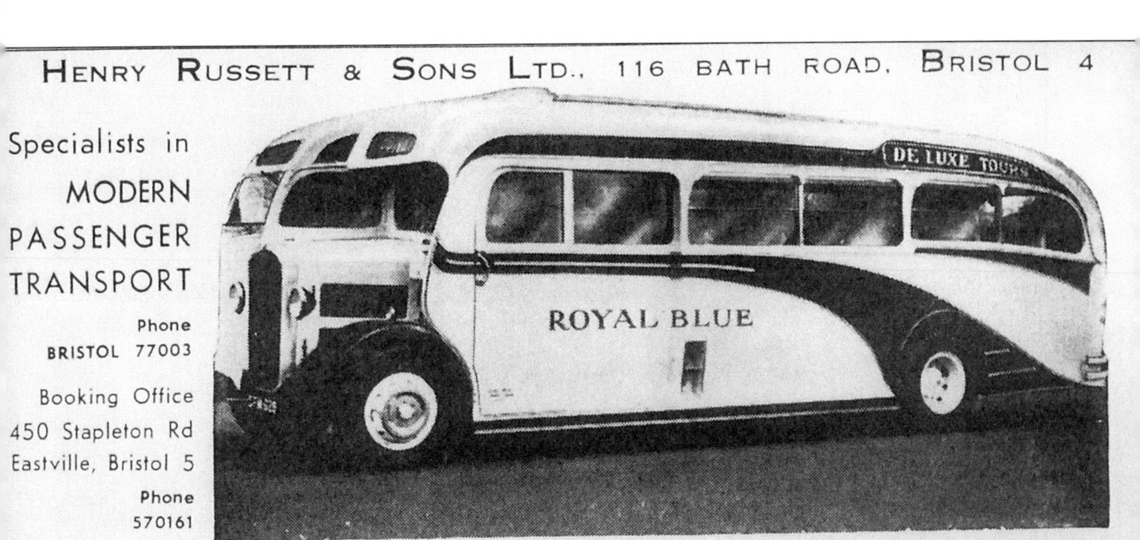

The Russett family have been involved in transport in Bristol since the 1860s. Henry Russett had a depot at Bath Road, Totterdown, which housed his fleet of lorries and coaches. The coaches were operated under the fleet name 'Royal Blue'– not to be confused with the famous Elliott Brothers' 'Royal Blue Express Services' of Bournemouth. A modern-looking coach is pictured in this advertisement from the late 1930s.

In 1950, after the haulage business of Henry Russett and Sons was acquired by the Road Haulage Executive, the eight Bedford and one Foden coach of Royal Blue were bought by Bristol Tramways. MHT597 was a 1949 Bedford OB with Duple coachwork. The coach was given the fleet number 289 and is seen here in Queen Square in the early 1950s.

Leyland charbanc LX8984 belonged to Morning Star Motors, owned by E. Jones and Sons Ltd. Mr Jones commenced charabanc operations in 1919 and, by the early 1920s, had established several express and local excursion services as well as a private hire and taxi operation. This charabanc is seen in Ducie Road, Barton Hill, parked opposite the Morton House tavern, just prior to an excursion in around 1925. The vehicle is fitted with pneumatic tyres.

Wessex Coaches Ltd were formed in August 1947. The vehicle pictured here was either EHY798 or EHY799, an Opel Blitz 8W with Duple coachwork, built in 1938 and formerly belonging to Clifton Greys. It is located outside the Wessex offices in Whiteladies Road, Clifton and is about to begin an afternoon tour to Cheddar Gorge. The Wessex livery of red and beige was to become famous all over the West Country.

On a bomb-site in Lawrence Hill, next to the Bunch of Grapes public house, Wessex Coaches established a coach station. The author remembers setting out on day trips from here in the late 1950s and early 1960s and especially remembers the Bedford SB coaches bumping their way over the rough ground.

The Bedford SB was the backbone of the Wessex coach fleet in the1950s and 1960s. This example, RUE 696, was acquired along with the business of G.F. Feltham and Son in 1961. Feltham operated under the name 'Kingswood Queen' and its coaches were painted blue and cream. RUE 696 was a Bedford SBG with Duple coachwork. Also acquired from Felthams was a large depot and offices at Moravian Road, Kingswood. This photograph was taken around 1955.

Advertisement for 'Queen of the Road' coaches, operated by the Bristol Co-operative Society, that appeared in the early 1950s. The Bristol Co-op began coach operations in 1927. They stopped during the Second World War and then started again in August 1947, after acquiring Gough's 'Queen of the Road' coaches – a company that dated back to before the 1920s. Gough's had a large depot at Stoke View Road, Fishponds, which also was taken over by the Co-op. In April 1963 Bristol Co-op sold its coach operation to Warners of Tewkesbury.

'Queen of the Road' NHY 637 on a day trip to Torquay and Paignton, c. 1952. This is a rare 1951 Sentinel SLC4, with Beadle centre-entrance coachwork. The vehicle's livery is dark green and pale green with the monogrammed initials 'BCS' on the sliding door. The coach behind is BMH 451, a 1934 Dennis, owned by Len Munden, who later founded Crown Coaches of Bristol.

In 1926, Alice and Herbie Ball started business in a converted barn in Goulter Street, repairing and hiring out bicycles and assembling them for the retail trade. By 1927, Mr Ball had acquired his first motor vehicle, a Model-T Ford, which acted as a charabanc at weekends. By 1934, the cycle side of the business finished and the name 'Eagle Coaches' was adopted. This view of Eagle's yard at Goulter Street shows CRN 856D, a 1966 Bedford VAM14, 783 JAE a 1960 Bedford SB1 and 419 THY, a 1963 Leyland Leopard L1. Eagle's livery at this time was red and cream. In 1986 Eagle moved to a new depot at Netham Road, Redfield.

In 1965 Princess Mary Coaches purchased EDD 685C, a Bedford SB with Duple Bella Vega coachwork. It was painted in Princess Mary's smart two-tone blue livery. The company was founded by S.G. Wiltshire in 1924 and had a depot in Soundwell Road. On 1 February 1983 Princess Mary sold out to Eagle Coaches, although the name was retained for a number of years after takeover. EDD 685C is now preserved and is seen here at the Bristol Festival of Transport in 1990.

JYD95 was a 1948 Leyland Tiger operated by Crown Coaches. The bodywork features lots of chrome, including a chrome-plated radiator. Crown Coaches was founded by Len Munden, a Bristolian ex-boxer, in 1953. Len was unique in that he was the first one-armed driver to gain a PSV licence. In 1977, Crown acquired Empress Coaches, together with its subsidary, Monarch Coaches. JYD 95 was painted red and cream.

SHY 124 was a 1954 AEC Reliance, owned by Empress of Bristol, and was painted in a cream and brown livery. The Empress Charabanc Co. was founded by A.H. Fielding in the early 1920s. In 1943 Rambler Coaches of Weston were acquired and in 1960 Empress merged with Monarch Coaches of Bristol. In 1977 A.H. Fielding died and the business and depot at Speedwell Road were sold to Len Munden and Sons.

J.W. and M.L. Sparkes traded as Sparkes Coaches and had a depot at The Grange, Deanery Road, Warmley. 884 HHW was a 1960 Bedford SB with Plaxton coachwork. Sparkes had a large fleet of second-hand coaches, used mainly on schools and works contracts. In the late 1970s the companies Sodbury Queen, Primrose Coaches, AD Coaches and Dons Coaches were all associated with Sparkes.

In the 1960s and early 1970s the Bedford VAL six-wheeled coaches were the longest coaches on the road. EDD883C was a 1965 model with Duple Vega Major bodywork and fifty-two seats. It was owned by Western Roadways, which was the fleet name used by A.W. Durbin since 1954. Durbin's company had a number of Bedford VALs, including four with the rare Caetano bodywork. Durbin's fleet of twenty-eight coaches were sold to Turners Coaches in 1979 and the red and cream livery disappeared in favour of a blue and white one.

In the early 1960s Bristol Omnibus revived the Greyhound name and all its coaches were painted cream and bright red with the name 'Bristol Greyhound' emblazoned along the sides. FHW 154D was delivered in 1966 and was a Bristol MW6G coach with Eastern Coachworks bodywork. The Greyhound coaches had their own garage building at Lawrence Hill Depot and were kept in immaculate condition. FHW 154D has been preserved.

On 1 August 1974 Wessex Coaches Ltd sold its express, excursion and tours licences, along with forty-two vehicles, to National Travel (South West) Ltd. This photograph, of LAE 892L, was taken outside of the Clifton Road garage on 29 July 1974. It was one of the last batch of new vehicles delivered to Wessex in 1973 and was a Bedford YRQ with Duple coachwork.

Seven
On The Buses

Bristol Tramways commenced motor bus operations in 1906 with a batch of twelve Thornycroft double-deckers, but only as a feeder service to the tramway system. Dissatisfied with their performance, Bristol started building its own vehicles at Filton in 1908. The ageing trams were replaced between 1938 and 1941 with 272 Bristol K-type double-deckers. The bus building side of the business became a separate company named Bristol Commercial Vehicles in 1955 and Bristol Tramways changed its name to the Bristol Omnibus Company in 1957.

As a child in the 1950s, travelling on the buses was part of everyday life, yet every trip was an adventure. I loved to sit in the seat behind the driver and watch him turn that big white steering wheel. At some stage the conductor would appear with a rack full of coloured tickets, to me these were prized possessions which I would take home to use with my conductor's set.

The Bristol Omnibus Company main offices at Bristol City Centre in the 1970s. To older Bristolians, these buildings are still known as the Tramway Offices. Before the Second World War, the city centre was called the Tramways Centre and these offices, along with the famous clock, belonged to the Bristol Tramway Company. In 1978 the offices were closed and moved to Berkeley House, Lawrence Hill.

PUBLIC NOTICES.

THE BRISTOL TRAMWAYS AND CARRIAGE COMPANY, LIMITED.

NEW MOTOR CHARABANC ROUTES

ON AND AFTER MONDAY, SEPTEMBER 16, 1912. MOTOR CHARABANCS WILL RUN HOURLY BETWEEN

TRAMWAYS CENTRE AND ST. JOHN'S LANE

(Terminus ENGINEERS' ARMS).

From CITY—Via Bristol Bridge, Victoria Street, York Road, St. Luke's Road, and St. John's Lane.
To CITY—Via St. John's Lane, Bushy Park, Wells Road Junction, Joint Station, and Bristol Bridge.

TO CITY, Every Hour. TIME TABLE.

ST. JOHN'S LANE (Engineers' Arms) to TRAMWAYS CENTRE, first 8.45 a.m., last 10.45 p.m.
BUSHY PARK CARS to TRAMWAYS CENTRE ... first 8.52 a.m., last 10.52 p.m.
JOINT STATION to TRAMWAYS CENTRE ... first 8.58 a.m., last 10.58 p.m.

FROM CITY, Every Hour.

TRAMWAYS CENTRE to ST. JOHN'S LANE ... first 9.15 a.m., last 11.15 p.m.
BRISTOL BRIDGE to ST. JOHN'S LANE ... first 9.18 a.m., last 11.18 p.m.
JOINT STATION to ST. JOHN'S LANE ... first 9.22 a.m., last 11.22 p.m.
On SUNDAYS—From ST. JOHN'S LANE ... first 2.45 p.m., last 9.45 p.m.
From TRAMWAYS CENTRE ... first 2.15 p.m., last 10.15 p.m.

See Detailed Time Tables for fuller information as to all intermediate stations.

FARES (either way):

Tramways Centre to St. Luke's Road (Hill Avenue) ... 1d
York Road Footbridge to St. John's Lane Terminus ... 1d
St. John's Lane Terminus to Wells Road Tramway Junc. ... 1d
Bushy Park Cars to Tramways Centre ... 1d

(Either way) Tramways Centre and St. John's Lane, 2d.

This Route is the nearest way to Lower Knowle, Lower Totterdown, Victoria Park, and Windmill Hill districts.

ALSO BETWEEN

OLD MARKET CAR TERMINUS and BARTON HILL

(THE BATHS, MAZE STREET)

Via West Street, Clarence Road, Barrow Road, Barton Hill Road, and Maze Street.

TO OLD MARKET. TIME TABLE. TO BARTON HILL.

From BARTON HILL to OLD MARKET, first 8.30 a.m., last 11.30 p.m. At the hour and half-past the hour. From STAFFORD STREET to OLD MARKET, first 8.33 a.m., last 11.33 p.m.

From OLD MARKET to BARTON HILL, first 8.15 a.m., last 11.15 p.m. At quarter-past and quarter-to the hour. From TRINITY CHURCH to BARTON HILL, first 8.19 a.m., last 11.19 p.m.

Fare, ONE PENNY, the whole or any part of the distance.

By this Route, nearest way to the whole of Barton Hill; the Footbridge for Feeder Road and St. Philip's Marsh; Netham Road; Newbridge Road for New Brislington; St. Anne's District. Connecting at Old Market with Electric Car and Motor 'Bus Services to all parts of the City and Suburbs.

Punctuality is not guaranteed but every endeavour will be made to ensure it.

FOR BLUE TAXI-CABS, Tel. No. 335.

Tramways Centre, September, 1912. CHARLES CHALLENGER, Manager.

Whenever the Bristol Tramway Company opened new routes, flyers were produced to advertise the service. This one, from September 1912, is promoting a new motor charabanc route from the Tramways Centre to St Johns Lane and Old Market to Barton Hill. The Barton Hill route later became part of route thirty-six and is now the only bus route in Bristol that still bears its original number.

One of the first twelve buses in Bristol, the Thornycroft Type 80 double-decker. They were registered AE725 to AE736. They operated on the tram feeder service from the Victoria Rooms to the suspension bridge, which commenced on 1 January 1906.

Within a year of their inception, the Thornycroft double-deckers were rebuilt as single-decker buses (charabancs). This one is AE727, which had thirty-two seats. It operated from Westbury to Redland, where it connected with the tram service to the Tramways Centre.

Bristol Tramways had competition from Charles Russett's Pioneer Company and Greyhound on the city routes. Pioneer started the first route from Barton Hill to Old Market and when Fishponds housing estate was opened in the 1920s, they started a new route to it from Old Market. Driver Tom Cunningham and his conductor are featured in this photograph, standing beside HT4358 at the Fishponds terminus. The body of the bus was built at Morrish and Sons, coachbuilders of Clarence Road, Bedminster in 1921 by Fred Arthur and Les Morse on a wartime Dennis chassis. Pioneer was sold to Greyhound in 1929.

Greyhound operated several city bus routes, including route twenty-two from Sea Mills to Bedminster Down, eighty-four from Tramways Centre to Downend and ninety-nine between Prince Street and Avonmouth. HY6198 was a 1932 Bristol G-type with Beadle bodywork: it looked very smart in Greyhound's white, grey and maroon livery. It is seen here at Colston Avenue on 12 January 1936 (although Greyhound had been fully absorbed by Bristol Tramways by 1 January 1936).

C2704 (CHU562) was delivered to Bristol Tramways in 1936 and was a Bristol JNW-type with Bristol dual-doorway bodywork. It is seen here after the war en route to Inns Court Road, Knowle. The 'C' prefix to the fleet number indicates that the vehicle was part of the Bristol City Services fleet which was operated jointly by Bristol Tramways and the Bristol Corporation.

Bristol L-type 2424 (HY1953) at the Lawrence Hill depot in the late 1950s. 2424 was originally a Bristol B-type built in 1930 and was rebuilt as an L-type in 1949.

Two fine-looking and well-preserved Bristol buses. On the left is C3336 (GHT154), a 1939 Bristol K-type painted in pre-war dark blue and white livery – the same as the trams. On the right is C4044 (LAE13), a 1947 Leyland Titan. Bristol had fifty Leyland Titans and allocated them all to the Eastville depot. Such was the shortage of materials after the war, that only a few had the chrome-plated radiators, the others having black-painted metal.

Up until 1961 Bristol buses carried the Bristol coat of arms. As the company did not want to pay money to the city council to use the official design, the company used its own and over the years several different versions were used. The arms includes the motto: 'Virtute et Industria'. This was replaced with 'BRISTOL' written in block letters and, later, by the famous Bristol scroll – the logo used by Bristol Commercial vehicles.

Bristol Tramways and Carriage Co. Ltd, opened a depot at Muller Road in 1946 to replace the old tram depot on Gloucester Road. It principally supplied vehicles for routes running up the busy Gloucester Road to Filton and Patchway. The picture looks to have been taken towards the end of, or soon after, the war as there are many women present. The vehicles in the background are Bristol K-types, the two on the left having wartime utility bodywork (the middle one being lowbridge). The one on the left is a tram replacement bus with Brislington bodywork.

Bristol K-type L3646 (HHY 590), outside the Bristol Tramways' office, situated next door to the Tatler cinema in Carey's Lane, Old Market, during the early 1950s. L3646 was built in 1945 and carries wartime utility bodywork built by Strachan. It was delivered in Tilling green and cream livery. The bus is on route 236 to Broomhill Road. The 'L' prefix indicates a lowbridge vehicle.

A view of C3177 (FHT 122) at the Sea Mills terminus of route 1C from Sea Mills to Brislington. The picture was taken in the early 1950s and the vehicle is in the Tilling green and cream livery that was adopted after the war. C3177 is a Bristol K5G with a BBW body, built in 1938.

Bristol K5G C3387 (JHT 803) at the Lawrence Hill depot in the late 1950s. The bus was built in 1946 and given new bodywork in 1950.

L8089 (OHY938) was one of a batch of ten Bristol KSW's with ECW lowbridge bodies delivered in 1952. They were the first double-deckers with platforms, doors and heaters. L8089 was owned by Bristol Tramways' subsidary, Bath Tramways Motor Company, for lowbridge routes in the Bath and Devizes area. In 1968 it was converted to a driver-training bus. In 1974 it was acquired by a good friend of the author, Peter Davey, for preservation. It is seen in 1992, about to work a trip for the Barton Hill History Group. Peter sold the vehicle recently to another preservationist.

Bristol KSW type C8240 (SHW410) at the Haymarket on route thirteen to Briar Way, The Downs, in the late 1950s. It is being passed by another KSW on the route and a Co-op, Morris J-type, bread van. Route thirteen later became Briar Way to Bedminster. C8240 was a Bristol KSW6B built in 1955 with a standard ECW highbridge body.

Bristol LD6B Lodekka type LC8271 (UHY398) outside the Bristol Tramways' office in Careys Lane, Old Market. LC8271 was built in 1955 to replace the older side-gangway lowbridge buses working the thirty-six and two-three-six routes. Lowbridge buses were necessary because of the railway bridge in West Town Lane. The Lodekka was revolutionary as it had a full-size body and did away with the need for a side gangway upstairs, as was normal on lowbridge vehicles.

Old buses never die, they just fade away. That can truly be said about FAE60, a 1938 Bristol L5G type. It started life as fleet number 2086 in the bus fleet. It was rebuilt in 1956 as a tree-topper and survived in service at the Lawrence Hill depot until the 1970s. It is seen here leaving Bristol bus station in the early 1960s.

This is the Bristol Tramways' depot at Avonmouth, built in 1915. It only ever housed buses. In 1949 Bristol Tramways operated 1,227 buses and there were depots at Lawrence Hill, Staple Hill, Muller Road, Winterstoke Road, Brislington, Hanham, Eastville and Avonmouth.

Bristol SUS4A type 305 (845THY) passing the Crown and Dove public house on route eighty from Bristol bus station to Dundry. This particular route ran through some very narrow lanes. The SUS was a smaller than normal single-decker and replaced the Bristol Omnibus Bedford OBs. The Dundry route was acquired in 1950 by Bristol Tramways from S.A and W.F. Ball, who traded as Dundry Pioneer. This was the last independent bus route in the city until deregulation in the 1980s.

Bristol LD6G L8541 (431 FHW) is leaving the back of Bristol bus station on 13 July 1972 on route 327 between Bristol and Frampton Cotterell. Bristol bus station was opened in 1958 on a large site, which included the former tramway depot in Whitson Street. The bus station also included a depot with full maintenance facilities. It was built with two platforms linked by a subway but later rebuilt with just one platform. A small BMC van (NHU 313F) belonging to the bus company is in the doorway.

When the Bristol FLF was introduced in 1960 it was revolutionary because it had a front entrance with driver-operated doors. The author first rode on them in the early 1960s when they operated the 311 Bristol bus station to Bitton route. These buses gradually took over on many city routes. In 1967 a new batch, delivered to the Winterstoke Road depot, took over the number nine route, one of these being the brand new C7298 (JHW 66E) which can be seen driving between Hanham and Ashton Drive in this photograph.

Eight
Kings of the Road

The first motor lorries appeared in Bristol in the early 1900s. After the First World War, surplus army lorries abounded and many new operators sprang up. By the mid 1930s vehicle design had greatly improved, culminating in the big rigid eight-wheelers. Following the Second World War, road haulage was nationalised. British Road Services was formed to absorb 4,000 concerns and 40,000 vehicles. BRS replaced the worst of the vehicles it inherited with new Bristol-built lorries. The industry was later denationalised.

My own memories of commercial vehicles begin in the late 1950s when red-liveried BRS lorries and green-liveried BRS parcel vans abounded. These were also the days when red and cream British Railways' three-wheelers made local deliveries, electric milk floats and bread vans delivered daily and coal was brought by flatbed lorries.

Robertsons were famous for their marmalade, which they made at their factory in Brislington. They also operated a fine fleet of Austin delivery vans. From left to right: KHU 308, JHY 291, HHU 931, JHW836, KHT 460, HHY 508, KHY 156 and LAE 230. This photograph was taken around 1948.

Bristol Corporation lorry HU 3291 is seen here somewhere in Bristol. This busy scene includes tram lines, a wooden council handcart and a laundry cart being pulled by a young boy. The vehicle appears to be a Model-T Ford, built in 1924.

William Henry Little stands beside another Bristol Corporation lorry, *c.* 1927. The vehicle is a Morris Commercial.

A Bristol four-ton lorry built in 1920 and exhibited at the Commercial Motor Show of that year. It was subsequently used by Bristol Tramways from 1923 to 1931 before being sold to a showman who used it until the early 1950s. It has been fully restored since then and is seen here at the Bitton Transport Rally in 1984.

G.H. Hill was a fruit and potato merchant based at Lawrence Hill. He garaged his fleet of lorries at the old Morning Star Motors depot. The sign for Morning Star is still above the garage entrance in this photograph, taken in the late 1920s. The vehicle to the right of the entrance is a Leyland.

PIONEER TRANSPORT LTD.

ROAD TRANSPORT SPECIALISTS

Controlling : S. J. Cox & Son, The Cross, STREET, Somerset
J. & T. Godfrey, Temple Street, KEYNSHAM, Somerset
Sharpness Transport Co. Ltd., High Street, BERKELEY, Glos.

LORRIES AND VANS TO SUIT ALL PURPOSES — MACHINERY AND ALL HEAVY HAULAGE — CONTRACTS ARRANGED

SERVICES
LONDON SOUTH COAST AND BRISTOL
POOLE BOURNEMOUTH
SOUTHAMPTON SALISBURY
THE NORTH OF ENGLAND
THE MIDLANDS AND SOUTH WALES; also in the following Counties : GLOS., WILTS., DORSET AND SOMERSET

DEPOTS :	TELEPHONES :
	Head Office : Bristol 57038 (3 lines)
ROSEMARY ROAD, NEWTOWN, PARKSTONE, DORSET	Parkstone 2099
27 PEEL GROVE, BETHNAL GREEN, LONDON, E.2	Advance 2746
THE CROSS, STREET, SOMERSET	Street 30
HIGH STREET, BERKELEY, GLOUCESTER	Berkeley 53
TEMPLE STREET, KEYNSHAM, SOMERSET	Keynsham 27

DRY SPACIOUS WAREHOUSES **VEHICLES OF ALL SIZES**

HEAD OFFICE :

46 DAY'S ROAD, ST. PHILIP'S, BRISTOL 2

An advertisement for Pioneer Transport, 1944.

Pioneer Transport No. 54 (BMX 114), was a Scammell rigid eight-wheeler built in 1935. These vehicles were the kings of the road from the 1930s to the 1950s. This lorry's livery was red with the words 'Pioneer Transport for heavy haulage' written across the front.

In 1933 Harold Russett left Pioneer Transport, taking the parcels and distribution side of the business with him to form Premier Transport. Premier Transport No. 17 (GHT 890), was an Austin K-Type and is seen here at the company's garage in Cumberland Street, St Philips. The vehicles are painted bright red and cream. A particularly nice touch is the list of destinations, that were operated daily from Bristol, written on the van body.

In the 1950s Premier Transport adopted a green livery. This fine line up of Austin lorries at the Sussex Street depot consists of: XHY 477, XHY 390, XHU 334, XHY 389 and XHW 628 – all delivered in 1956. Premier Transport are still in business today, although this part of the depot is now occupied by Wessex National Ltd.

KNEE BROS. (BRISTOL) LTD.

16 Temple Street
Bristol 1

TELEPHONE 26611

OFFER AN UNEQUALLED SERVICE IN LOCAL, LONG DISTANCE OR OVERSEAS REMOVALS, PACKING FOR SHIPMENT, STORAGE, ETC.

Depositories : **BOYCE'S AVENUE, CLIFTON, BRISTOL 8.** Telephone 33548

London Agents : **Bishop & Sons Depositories Ltd., 10-12 Belgrave Road, S.W.1**

Knee Bros. (Bristol) Ltd advertisement, late 1930s. The vehicle is BHY 429, a 1935 Bedford.

For Reliable Transport Consult—

H. W. HAWKER LTD.

ALBERT ROAD, ST. PHILIP'S, BRISTOL, 2

'Phone 77047-8

Lancashire Depot : 60 SUTTON STREET, WARRINGTON. *'Phone 1413*

H.W. Hawker Ltd had depots at Bristol and Warrington and operated a daily service from Bristol to Lancashire and the South Coast. This solid looking eight-wheeler is magnificently lettered and painted. The advertisement is from the 1930s.

Crossing the railway line at Warmley is one of only two Scammell 100-tonners ever made. KD 9168 was built in 1929 for Marston Road Services. In 1937 it was acquired by Edward Box and Co. of Liverpool, together with its special trailer, which was fitted with rails for carrying railway engines. In this photograph it is seen hauling a load that originated from Metropolitan Vickers of Trafford Park in Manchester. In 1949 KD9168 joined the other 100-tonner, BLH 21, in the Pickfords Fleet.

In the mid 1930s George's Brewery operated this fine fleet of Thornycroft petrol lorries. They are seen here, fully laden, at the Bath Street Brewery. Note the slogan 'Beer is best' on the front two. AHY 596 was registered in 1934.

This fine example of a GMC troop carrier evokes many wartime memories. Many American troops were stationed in the Bristol area during the latter part of the Second World War and vehicles such as this one became a familiar sight. It was photographed at Church Road, St George on 2 July 1996 after its repatriation to England, only yards away from the wartime St George Civil Defence Headquarters.

During the Second World War, Fry's converted this 1934 van into an emergency canteen. BAE 290 has masked headlight and white-painted mudguards, which were compulsory to comply with blackout regulations. The canteen is seen here outside the Somerdale factory at Keynsham.

GHY 730 was a 1940 ambulance, owned by the St John Ambulance Brigade, used for the transport of Bristol Contributory Scheme Welfare Association members. This vehicle also has masked headlights.

Lorry drivers and staff employed by the Co-ordinated Traffic Services, pose outside the Bristol office at the old Great Western cotton factory premises in Maze Street, Barton Hill, around 1945.

A Ford E83W van parked outside the Carpenters Arms by St James churchyard near the corner with Bond Street, 7 April 1952. Small traders and companies quickly realised that little vans could reach a large customer area. A great variety of small delivery vans were produced from the 1930s onwards.

JHU 236 was an Austin van built in 1946 and owned by Arthur Scull and Sons Ltd. It is seen here outside the Greyhound Hotel in Broadmead on 22 October 1952. The Greyhound Hotel was one of Bristol's old coaching inns and managed to survive the blitz. The scaffolding to the right is the new Broadmead in the process of being constructed around the Greyhound.

This unusual vehicle operated in the goods yard at Midland Road. HYK 602 was registered in London in 1947.

MTV 878 is a Reliant motorcycle van, built in 1950. It is preserved and owned by J. Goodfield and Sons, General Builders, Chipping Sodbury and is seen here at Ashton Court. These three-wheeled delivery vans became popular in the 1930s, a time when local retailers competed fiercely for the delivery service market.

BRITISH ROAD SERVICES

Central Bristol Group—GENERAL HAULAGE.

CHEESE LANE
BRISTOL, 2

Telephone 23521

Nightly Services TO MIDLANDS AND NORTH

AREAS SERVED

The whole of Scotland, the whole of Lancashire and Yorkshire and the North of England, plus the West Midlands (Birmingham, Wolverhampton, etc.) including the Black Country.

East Bristol Group—GENERAL HAULAGE—Special Vans.

46 DAYS ROAD
BRISTOL, 2

Telephone 58481

Nightly Services TO LONDON

AREAS SERVED

The whole of the South Eastern Counties, including London. The Eastern Counties. The East Midland area including Leicester, Notts, and Derby plus the major portion of the Counties of Worcester, Gloucester, Oxford, Berkshire and Wiltshire.

South Bristol Group—GENERAL HAULAGE—TIPPERS.

116 BATH ROAD
BRISTOL, 4

Telephone 77003

Nightly Services TO SOUTHAMPTON

Avonmouth Dock Office, Tel. Av. 385

AREAS SERVED

The South of England to a point approximately 20 miles North and East of Southampton. Mid. and South Wales plus the Western Part of the Counties of Shropshire and Hereford.

NOTE. Within a road distance of 35 miles of Bristol there is an Area which is non-directional to the three Groups in question.

Bristol Parcels Group.

2 ALBERT ROAD
BRISTOL, 2

Telephone 77691

SERVICES

There is a Countrywide service operating from this Group for normal Parcels and "Smalls" consignments up to one ton in weight.

After the nationalisation of Bristol haulage companies by the goverment, they became part of British Road Services. Former rival companies were grouped together. This local advertisement from the 1950s makes interesting reading; the Bristol Parcels Group included the former companies Carter Patersons and Pickfords.

In the nationalisation of the road haulage industry, the government started to acquire companies, both large and small. Many of the vehicles, especially from the smaller operators, were old and could only be described as 'bangers'. BRS started a vehicle replacement program and introduced its own designs, built by Bristol Commercial Vehicles with bodies by Longwell Green Coachworks. YAE 128 is a Bristol HA-type, dating from 1957. As it belonged to the parcel side of BRS it is in green livery and carries the fleet number RF171.

From the general haulage side of BRS operations is UFJ 691, a 1956 Albion FT37 with the famous rising-sun emblem on the radiator. The vehicle is in the general haulage fleet's red livery and carries the number 6G152, indicating that it belonged to the Exeter depot.

Ford E83W lorry KYD 245, now preserved and owned by Saunders and Ralph of Bristol. Seen here at Ashton Court, the van was built in 1949

The most famous name in ice cream around Bristol is Verrecchia's (although Bristolians pronounce the name 'Vereesha's'). They operated, until recently, a fleet of vintage Morris J-type ice cream vans, such as 846 EHT which was built in 1959. The vans were painted either pink and cream as is this one, or light green and cream. The location of this scene is Tog Hill, just outside of Bristol.

S. & A. Stone Ltd is a long-established Bristol haulage contractor. In the familiar 'stone' livery of chocolate and black is DFH 933, a preserved 1939 Bedford O-type, which was the archetypal haulage and coal merchant's lorry of the 1940s and 1950s.

LYO 779 is a 1951 Bedford S-type. It is owned by John Shipp, a haulage merchant of Thornbury and is seen here at the North Nibley steam rally, 31 May 1992. The North Nibley event is held every year.

Very nearly a hundred years before this old photograph was taken, the name of FISH was established in Bristol haulage.

The firm's unbroken history carries it through the horse days, to steam, and now to the modern type of vehicle pictured below.

The service we offer is given by a fleet of vehicles maintained at a high level of mechanical efficiency and appearance, operated by a permanent team of drivers, many of whom have been with us well over 30 years.

We feel that such a background, coupled with our policy always to offer the best in transport, is of the very essence of this PRIVATE ENTERPRISE, of which we are proud to be a part.

JOSEPH FISH & SONS Ltd.

1-3 PEEL STREET, PENNYWELL ROAD, BRISTOL 5

Phone 5-6061-2

An advertisement for Joseph Fish and Sons Ltd, that appeared in 1956. The author remembers the depot at Peel Street in the late 1950s and early 1960s as being full of dark green-liveried Bedford lorries. The modern lorry in the advertisement is TAE 897, a Bedford S-type articulated vehicle, built in 1954.

LHY 584 is a 1947 Fordson lorry, belonging to Holders haulage contractors of Portishead. It is now preserved and this photograph was taken at the Bristol Festival of Transport, held at Hergrove Park.

Many of Joseph Fish and Sons' loads originated at Bristol or Avonmouth docks. OAE 394, a 1951 Bedford O-type, is seen here being loaded at Bristol Docks in 1958. Another O-type waits behind.

37 DHU was a 1958 Ford Thomas Trader, owned by Western Transport whose Bristol depot was at Feeder Road. A list of other Western Transport depots can be seen on the vehicle. It is painted a dark green colour and has red mudguards.

NFD 44 was a 1952 Scammell Highwayman, owned by Plant Transport and Installation of Bath, who had depots in both Bath and Bristol. The Scammell is seen here setting out from Stothert and Pitt in around 1965 with an outside load, consisting of a crane cab, going to Avonmouth Docks. The driver is Les Heron from St George in Bristol. He was formerly a driver for E.W. Badman and Sons who transferred to P.T.I.. After they acquired Badmans in 1964, P.T.I. were owned by Sparrows the crane specialists.

William Butler and Co. (Bristol) Ltd had a large tar works at Crews Hole. In the 1950s Butlers bought a fleet of International articulated tankers to replace the barges. SHY 109 is seen here loading at Crews Hole in 1958. The vehicle was registered in 1954. International was an American manufacturer and their vehicles were quite a rare sight in Bristol until the arrival of the Butlers' fleet.

Land Rovers make very useful small recovery vehicles. The Bristol Omnibus Company owned this 1972 example, FAE 778K. The livery is orange and cream with the famous Bristol Scroll, as seen on the buses, painted on the side. It was based at the company's Lawrence Hill depot and is pictured here passing The Eglington public house (later renamed The Seahorse) in Upper Maudlin Street on 13 July 1972, on its way to a breakdown.

AAE 310J is a Leyland with an ergomatic cab. It belonged to Bristol Steel Corporation, Chemicals Division, and is seen here at the old Butler's tar works at Crews Hole, which by 1970 had become part of British Steel. This type of cab had become standard for British Leyland and could be seen on Leyland, AEC and Albion lorries, making them all look the same.

BHW 432 is a remarkable vehicle. It started life as a Bristol Tramways' bus and entered service in 1935. It is a Bristol J-type. In 1960 it was sold by the bus company to George Rogers, who converted it to fairground use and travelled in it for some years, before selling it to Mrs Alice Hardiman and her son, Freddie. For thirty-four years it transported their stalls and towed the family's living wagon around Bristol and the West Country. The Hardimans named it 'The Masterpiece', after the famous Burrell engine owned by John Cole, Alice's grandfather. It passed into preservation in 1995.

The Leyland Octopus was a popular eight-wheeler produced from the 1930s to the 1960s. 522 DXL is a 1962 model which has had a large covered body built onto it for the transportation of A. Mander and Son's ghost train ride. It is seen here behind the ride at Clevedon in the mid 1970s.

Wynn's fair operated this AEC mark V eight-wheeler to carry part of its dodgem ride. 945 DFW was built in 1963 and also carries a generator built at the back end. Eight-wheelers have always found favour in the fairground: many were converted from petrol tankers. The location of this photograph is Bedminster Down at the annual summer fair in the mid 1970s.

Many fine British-built lorries were still to be found on the fairground in the early 1990s. WMP 479G was a 1969 six-wheel Atkinson, belonging to Bob Wilson's fun fair. It carries a generating plant and is seen here powering one of the many rides on Durdham Downs at the, then annual, Easter funfair. Note the frontal drawbar which enables the positioning of trailers and caravans on the fairground.

GHW 415 was built in 1938 and is a Leyland Turntable Escape fire engine, supplied new to Bristol Police Fire Brigade. It was based at Bridewell Fire Station. In 1939 it moved to Salisbury and was repainted in N.F.S grey in 1941. After the war it reverted to the red livery and remained in service at Salisbury until 1968. It is now preserved and is seen here at the Bristol Festival of Transport in 1995.

Bristol Central Ambulance Station at Tower Hill was completed in October 1966. SHU 573G is a 1968 BMC ambulance painted in a silver livery. It is now preserved and is still garaged at Tower Hill.

Nine

Get Out and Get Under

The invention of the internal combustion engine changed not only our transport demands, but also our whole way of life. Cars gradually evolved from the very primitive machines of the 1890s and early 1900s into more reliable vehicles. However, cars were expensive and before the First World War they could only be afforded by the wealthy. Early cars were prone to lots of breakdowns, so tools had to be carried to deal with any problems that arose. Furthermore, roads were very poor by today's standards and there were no petrol stations. After the First World War things improved: many men had become familiar with motorised transport in the armed forces and, as car ownership spread, set up repair garages to keep them in working order. Henry Ford's Model-T was mass produced and cheap and enabled more people to own cars. This, in turn, led to the creation of the petrol station.

Bristol's first number plate, AE1, adorned this 1904 Clement owned by Mr and Mrs Thomas Butler (owners of Butler's tar works). They are seen here on an outing with friends. Number plates were first introduced under the Motor Car Act of 1903 which required that from 1 January 1904 every car should be registered with a county or borough council and that every vehicle should have its own individual number. AE1 now adorns the Lords Mayor's official car.

When cars first appeared there were no garages. Petrol was sold in chemist's shops and repairs were often carried out by blacksmiths. Eventually, after the First World War, small garages began to appear. This picture shows the Lawrence Hill garage of Lines and Sons. The garage offered motor repairs, cars for hire, taxis and cycle repairs, plus petrol at 1s 4½d (7p per gallon).

In its infancy, Bristol Tramways provided many services in addition to trams. These included haulage, removals, taxis and even funeral services. The first motor cabs began operations in 1908 and eventually over 300 were in service. They were of French manufacture, either Charron or Clement-Bayard, and were operated under the fleetname 'Blue Motor Cabs'. This excellent picture comes from a company advert. The cabs were sold by auction in 1930 at an average price of £2 10s each.

Charles Russett operated taxis as well as charabancs and motor lorries. AE 7228 is probably of French manufacture. Behind it stands Pioneer No. 1, AE 6639, which was a Pierce Arrow three-ton charabanc, built in 1916. In 1929 it was rebuilt as a lorry for the haulage fleet. The location of this photograph is Russett's depot at Days Road, which later became the British Road Services depot in the 1950s.

Many young men returned from the First World War having learned to drive and wanted cars of their own. However, cars were still the province of the affluent. This magnificent 1921 Vauxhall was owned by the manager of the Bristol Wagon and Carriage Works. The chauffeur is Mr Houghton. The 1920s saw the construction of some of the finest luxury cars ever made.

This garage in High Street, Hanham was owned by Bence and Sons Ltd, who operated a network of local bus routes radiating from Hanham. Bence Motor Services was later acquired by Bristol Tramways in 1936. Over the years the depot was enlarged and modernised, but it eventually closed in 1981. Bence Motor Services was founded by William Bence, as was Longwell Green Coachworks, which continued until 1983. This photograph was taken around 1920.

A typical early petrol station built in the late 1920s. This is Hambrook garage on the main Bristol to Gloucester road. The garage is constructed of galvanised sheeting and wood and is of a barn-type construction. When this picture was taken, in the 1950s, the pumps were selling Shell, National and BP petrol as well as Castrol oil.

Car design improved steadily, using lessons learned from motor sport. By the 1930s, prices had fallen and cars became more widely available. BHU 896 was a 1935 Austin. Production of private cars ceased during the Second World War and afterwards for some years it was an export-only industry. This meant that in the 1950s there were plenty of 1930s cars still around. Roy King, a young driver, is dwarfed by the size of this car.

Broadmead in pre-pedestrianised days. This picture was taken on 3 November 1952, shortly after Woolworths was opened. There are plenty of cars in this picture, as well as push-bikes and two interesting commercial vehicles. GYV 486 is a 1944 Royal Mail delivery van and is being passed by a Fordson lorry belonging to Thomas Cox and Sons, builders merchants.

In the 1950s, parking in the town was no problem. The whole area was littered with cleared bomb-sites which presented ample parking opportunities. A typical variety of cars of the period can be seen here: LAE 266 is a 1947 Austin 10, PHT 311 is a 1952 Morris Minor 1000, whilst two pre-war boneshakers, a Ford Prefect and a Bedford O-type lorry (belonging to S.H. Parker and Son Ltd, glass manufacturers), are parked to their right. The location is Barrs Street, looking towards the rear of Regent Terrace.

Parked outside The Antelope public house at no. 34, Broadmead on 23 July 1953 are GHT 543, a 1939 Ford Anglia EO4A two-door saloon (still with white-painted blackout mudguards) and ST6644, a large 1.5 litre Riley.

Wilder Street, St Pauls, early 1960s. From left to right: FHY 607 (a 1939 Ford Prefect 4-door saloon), a Standard 10, a Bristol Dairies hand-steered electric milk float, NHU 736 and DLK 312. In the background is a Power petrol tanker.

Whiteladies Road, Clifton, 20 July 1956. The cars parked outside the shops are as follows: KYC 490 is a 1948 Austin Devon four-door saloon, PHW 838 is a 1952 Hillman Minx Phase V four-door saloon and the van, owned by George Davis (Clifton) Ltd, is a Ford E83W.

A fine line-up of cars in Charlton Street, Lawrence Hill on 3 July 1964. Looking from left to right we see: the rear of a Morris Minor, NHU 636 (a 1950 Ford Prefect four-door saloon) and SJH 56 (a 1954 Ford Popular two-door saloon). A Vauxhall Victor four-door saloon is parked outside the Charlton Gospel Hall. In the background can be seen the Barrow Road bridge, the top of Barrow Road engine shed and the Days Road gasworks.

FHT 18 is a beautifully-preserved 1938 Austin 7 two-door saloon, painted emerald green with black mudguards and grill. This make of car, introduced in 1922, was a revolutionary design and made a fortune for Austin. This photograph was taken at Ashton Court.

GHU 64 is a Ford Anglia two-door saloon. This car provided excellent go-anywhere post-war transportation, offering a top speed of sixty mph and the economy of thirty to thirty-five mpg. Unfortunately these benefits came with considerable discomfort. This car survives, in immaculate condition, with the customary black paint scheme and was pictured here at Oldbury Court in 1995.

PDG 312 was a 1955 Ford Zephr One. It is basically a Consul with a different grill, two extra cylinders, unitary construction, upstairs valves, MacPherson struts and hydraulic brakes. When properly tuned it could give Jaguar-like performance but not comparable handling. The car is passing Lloyds Bank in North Street, Stokes Croft, not far behind an Austin 1100. The photograph was taken in 1963.

A fine pair of Vauxhalls belonging to Lines and Sons taxis and wedding cars, at no. 30, Easton Road. On the left is SHT 862, a 1954 Vauxhall Cresta and on the right, THW 859, a 1954 Vauxhall Velox.

UHT 508 is a 1955 Vauxhall Cresta Epic. This car was Vauxhall's answer to the Ford Zodiac. It boasted such refinements as: leather trim, two-toning inside and out, heater, clock, mascot, lockable filler cap and rear wheel spats. This particular car has been beautifully preserved and is pictured here in the grounds of Ashton Court Estate.

932 DAE is a 1958 BMW Isetta, commonly known as a 'bubblecar', a type which was very popular in the early 1960s. Entry to the car was through a swinging front door. The engine is a BMW motorcycle unit. These cars were great fun with their two seats and sunroof. This photograph was taken at Ashton Court estate.

Line-up of vehicles in Cheltenham Road, mid 1970s. From left to right are: a Bedford HA van, 250 UHY, a 1963 Austin Cambridge A60 and a Ford Cortina Mark One. The author bought his first car from P.J. Motors.

The author's first car, a 1963 Hillman Minx 469 GXL, bought for £110 in 1972. It stands outside the family house at George Street, Redfield, complete with learner plates. The car was grey in colour, had a 1500 engine and was built like a tank. It was traded in, during 1974, for an almost-new Hillman Hunter with a 1725 engine.

Ten

On Two Wheels

The bicycle is the simplest form of road transport and the cheapest. The early bikes were strange affairs, especially the Penny Farthing, which was not only absurd in appearance but extremely dangerous to ride. The safety-cycle greatly improved matters.

The first motorcycles were slightly modified bicycles with engines fitted above the front or rear wheels. They used a belt drive and were very unstable. In 1901, Werner Brothers placed the engine where the pedals used to be and the modern motorcycle layout was created.

In Bristol at his Lawrence Hill workshop, P.J. Kerswell designed and built his own machines and in 1904 invented the detachable sidecar. Three years later, Douglas Brothers began making motorcycle parts at their factory at Kingswood, thus beginning Bristol's involvement in the British motorcycle industry.

Throughout the 1930s, 1940s and 1950s, Britain built the best motorcycles in the world. Advertisements like this one were produced to encourage the working man to get rid of his push-bike and purchase a new motorcycle. AJS, BSA, Douglas, Norton, Triumph, Royal Enfield, Superior and Velocette are all famous and evocative names from this era.

The West of England Meat Co. had a shop at West Street, Old Market. Like many other butchers and grocers, local deliveries were made by a boy on a push-bike. A large carrier and basket were fitted to the front of the bike for the goods. This photograph was taken around 1925.

Raleigh push-bike from the 1930s. Made in Nottingham, these bikes were solid and heavy. The three-speed sturmy-archer gears, pull-up brakes, Brookes saddle and Lucas 'King of the Road' bell were typical features. Sales of push-bikes flourished in the 1920s and 1930s and local cycling clubs were formed by enthusiasts.

Douglas bikes were special, because they were made in Bristol. This was unusual in itself as most of the big-name motorcycle manufacturers were in the Midlands or London. The first bikes were produced at the Kingswood factory in 1907. This image shows a 1913 vintage 2.75 hp, two-speed, belt drive, horizontally-opposed twin model. ET 708 was registered in Rotherham.

Jim Cox sits astride ER 3754. Note the solid leather boots, muffler and horn on the handlebars. The location is No. 10, Queen Ann Road, Barton Hill and the year is around 1925.

Douglas

As smooth as Birds on the Wing—

Here are two superb 500 c.c. dual purpose machines suitable for either solo or sidecar work, each giving the traditional smooth vibrationless running of the unique Douglas Motor Cycles.

Whether for the enthusiast touring under all conditions, or the rider needing a machine to take a sidecar without the least strain, these two 500c.c. models represent the ideal, giving consistently reliable performance, no matter what they are called upon to do.

If a machine of lesser power is required, we offer our model A.32 350c.c. S.V., or K.32 350c.c. O.H.V., either of which will be found to possess armchair comfort, no vibration, and silence.

The selection of a Douglas for your 1932 mount assures you of the most modern and advanced motor-cycle of the year. Why not take the first step to-day and send for our 1932 Catalogue which illustrates and details every model in the famous Douglas range.

THE CHEAPEST & BEST TWIN CYLINDER MACHINE ON THE MARKET.

£39 10s.

C.32 500c.c. S.V., under 224lb.

ELECTRIC LIGHTING £4 10s. extra.

TAX 30s.

A dual purpose machine suitable for solo or side-car work.

£45 10s.

M.32 500c.c. O.H.V. Touring.

ELECTRIC LIGHTING £5 10s. extra.

Douglas MOTORS, LTD., KINGSWOOD, BRISTOL

A 1932 advertisement for Douglas motorcycles.

Roy King sits proudly astride LHY 26, a 1949 BSA. This is a powerful machine which sports a fine compliment of chronium plating. During the 1950s increasing prosperity meant that young men, like Roy, could afford fine British-built machines like this one.

The 1950s was the heyday of the motorcycle combination: if you could not afford a car, then what better way to take your family for a day out? TK 3528 is attached to an open sidecar, which has been named 'Madeline'. Many sidecars were fully enclosed. The author remembers a trip to Exmouth, when he was a toddler, in a motorcycle combination carrying four adults and two children.

In the 1950s, Kings of Oxford had a motorcycle showroom on the corner of North Street and Cherry Lane. Above the door it states that over 300 new and used motorcycles are available. There is also an advertisement for Lambretta scooters and, ominously, an advertisement for Suzuki. Cheap Japanese motorcycles eventually sounded the death knell for the British bike industry. In this picture PKL 729, a 1952 Morris Minor, can be seen passing along North Street.

In 1951 Douglas Motorcycles began making Vespa motorscooters under licence. In 1957 Douglas stopped production of motor bikes but continued importing Vespas until the 1980s. During the 1950s scooters were popular with all age groups. The scooter was a fun machine and Bill Heath riding THW 724, built in 1955, is certainly game for a laugh on a family day out in the country. The Vespa was owned by his son-in-law Jack Williams and was purchased from Kings motorcycle dealers.